The Tartan Legend

THE TARTAN LEGEND

The Autobiography

Ken Buchanan

HEADLINE

First published in 2000
by HEADLINE BOOK PUBLISHING

10 9 8 7 6 5 4 3 2 1

British Library Cataloguing in Publication Data

Buchanan, Ken
    The tartan legend: the autobiography
    1.Buchanan, Ken
    2.Boxers (Sports) - Scotland - Biography
    I.Title
    796.8'3'092

ISBN 0 7472 7006 6

Typeset by
Letterpart Limited, Reigate, Surrey

Printed and bound in Great Britain by
Mackays of Chatham PLC, Chatham, Kent

HEADLINE BOOK PUBLISHING
A division of Hodder Headline
338 Euston Road
London NW1 3BH

www.headline.co.uk
www.hodderheadline.com

To my mum Cathy, who was called by God early in life, and who is always in my thoughts. And to my dad Tommy, who has always been there for me, sometimes as a dad, sometimes as a trainer, but always as a friend.

contents

introduction

We're all fighters, every single one of us. Fighting is the first
sport of every man and woman. From the minute we're born,
we're fighting to breathe. Then we're fighting to open our eyes.
We're fighting to walk and we're fighting to talk. You can't get rid
of your desire to fight when that is the very first lesson you learn
in life. It's just that some people hide it a lot better than others.

This is the story of my relationship with that urge to fight.
How it affected me and others round about me. I have made
mistakes in my life but I prefer not to dwell on them. I had it all.
Everything. There was the money from the boxing, a thriving
business, a wife and two kids, a lovely a house in an up-market
area of Edinburgh. I earned it all from fighting. But I lost a lot for
having that working-class disease of being too big-hearted – in
some walks of life that is a pure liability. But wait, don't write me
off as a bitter ex-boxer – hear what I've got to say, then make
your decision. Keep an open mind.

my first gloves and the brown bomber

Looking back now it can seem like destiny. If I had been always running about with a ball at my feet and become a famous footballer, people would probably have said, *Oh, he never had a ball away from his feet, it was obvious he was going to become a footballer.* But I know hundreds of guys who had balls at their feet and loads of ability, but only a couple became professional footballers. Life waylaid them en route.

As for the academic life – I didn't do too well. Think how I feel writing this book! Ken Buchanan M.B.E., the author. It just doesn't seem right, not right at all. I didn't do a thing at school. All I ever won at school were fights and the bible prize. Looking back, my life could have gone two ways. A minister or a boxer. Imagine me a minister, now that is a laugh. The Reverend Buchanan. So how did I come to choose boxing over the clerical life? Quite simple really – all I can tell you is the things I remember about those days. The things I think are important to my story.

As a kid I grew up in Northfield. It was just a stone's throw away from Portobello. We lived in a council house – actually it was referred to as a prefab. We had a garden which led down to the Figgate Burn Park. My first school was Towerbank primary. As I grew up most of our lunch breaks were spent playing football behind the bike sheds. It should have been one team of boys against another. But on many occasions I ended up fighting with one of the boys who was playing against me. The fight would be over whether or not the ball went over the 'bar'. There was no bar: just two piles of jumpers or jackets for the posts. So, as you can imagine, the height of the imaginary bar was forever in dispute. Another reason for arguing and fighting was if the other team moved one of its posts (pile of jumpers) in, so that their goal was narrower than ours. Everybody argued sometime or other, but it always seemed to be me that got into the fights.

It was just kids' stuff – pushing and pulling. Challenging. I could see that most of the kids were scared, but I got a buzz out of it, an adrenaline rush – although I never knew that's what it was at the time. I especially seemed to like squaring up to somebody much bigger than myself. I'd be right in there going head to head with these guys whether the argument was my fault or not. There were even times I would fight for someone else if I thought they were in for a belting. I would step in and take the fight myself. Looking back, I must have been off my head to be fighting other people's battles.

Considering none of my family were involved in boxing it has often been asked how I got involved. Well – that was the result of two coincidences.

My mum, Cathy, and my dad, Tommy, my brother, Alan, and myself were out Christmas shopping in December 1953. It was cold and wet and people in heavy coats were bumping into each other. My dad saw something and he lifted me up and pointed to a poster for a film about Joe Louis – 'The Brown Bomber'.

'Ken, look at that: Joe Louis. You and I'll have to go and see that,' he said.

Seeing as my brother Alan was only four, my mum took him home as it was getting late and my dad and myself jumped on a bus for Leith Walk to watch the picture in the Palace Picture House. A lot of people did not have tellies so the picture house was the only venue where one could watch the latest movies. So in we went, little knowing how this picture I was about to watch would mould me into the Champion I would become.

So when the curtains went back I was taken away to this other world. Transported. The gyms, the bags, the gloves and the fights in the ring. The close-ups of the nose snorting and the lips. The pure heroism of the boxers. That is what I wanted to be: a hero. Up there in the ring. There was something about the honesty of all that. You can't fake your ability in a boxing ring. You can't bullshit your way to the top like you can in a lot of other professions. You stand or fall by your own ability. I think that is what I saw in that film. Men living on their ability, relying on nobody but themselves. By the time that film was finished I knew that I wanted to be a boxer – even though I was only eight years old. And I knew something else: I wanted to be world champion.

Coming out of the cinema, I asked my dad if he'd take me to a boxing club, and he said he would. I asked him again. In the end, I must have asked him that question a million times on the way home, as well as asking him another million and a half questions about the film. But he'd done what dads do and promised me everything. In bed that night all I could think about was me up there in the ring, battered and bruised, cut, but battling my way to the world title. And the whole school watching as I take the trophy. Kenny Buchanan, world champion. Cameras flashing everywhere. A big cheer goes up and I fall asleep.

The other coincidence was my aunt Agnes. She knew nothing about my having decided to become world champion after the Joe Louis movie. At the weekend all the family would meet at my gran's house and my cousin Robert and me would usually end up fighting. Robert was a year older than me, taller and much heavier. He'd usually win because he'd trip me up and sit on me until my mum or his mum came and separated us. It was nearly Christmas so Robert's mum (my auntie Agnes) went out and bought two pairs of boxing-gloves. They were Christmas presents but she gave us them early. We were to be found every weekend from there on in sparring in the back garden, knocking lumps out of each other. Auntie Agnes buying those gloves and the Joe

Louis film were signs to me. If I had any doubts before, I had none now. None at all as we had a few rounds together. I don't know what was going through Robert's mind, but I was back in the title ring battling through a gruelling last round.

My dad had said he'd take me to a boxing club, but he still hadn't. He said he'd look for one, but he still hadn't done that either. It's crazy the way you think when you're a laddie. When my dad came home at night I'd imagine he had been out all day searching for a boxing club for me, but he'd only been at his work or visiting one of his mates. Every night I waited for the word, but he never mentioned it. Nothing happened for what seemed like ages and as an eight-year-old laddie it felt like years though it was probably only a couple of weeks. Then one day up the town I noticed that the Joe Louis poster was gone. It looked like the dream was over. It was a science-fiction film they were showing now. I had to pluck up the courage to ask him. I kept looking for the opportunity. An opening. I was hanging about my dad like a puppy. Then one day, while he was working in the garden, I pestered him about it, and cornered him at the hedge. There was no escaping this one.

'Dad, remember we went to the Joe Louis film?'

'Aye. Great that, wasn't it?'

'You said you would find me a boxing club!'

He promised he definitely would this time. I pestered him the rest of the day. Would he find one? Would he take me? He said, 'Yes, yes, yes, I said I'd find you one and I will.'

'Is that a promise?'

I remember he straightened up – his hand on the spade. 'Oh – aye,' he said.

'Is that a promise?'

'You already asked that! A million times.'

'But is it? A promise?'

'Aye, it's a promise!'

Yes! I knew I had him because my dad always told me never

make a promise and not keep it. That was one of the worst things you could do as an honest man: break a promise. All I had to do now was wait.

A couple of weeks later my dad got permission to bring me along to the Sparta Amateur Boxing Club in McDonald Road, Edinburgh. I was over the moon when he told me. And the name – Sparta – that sounded good. It was a great name for a boxing club. I have never come across another one as good as that since. Not in all my days in boxing. Sparta! That began a long, long affiliation between me and the Sparta Club.

The Sparta Club was where I was to train for all my amateur fights. Over the years I won everything from area titles to British titles. From the day I first went into Sparta, boxing was in my blood. And yet I was very nearly disappointed there and then. Mr Boyter, who was in charge of training the juniors, asked me my age. When I told him I was eight and a half years old he told my dad that they didn't start training juniors till they were at least nine. My heart sank. My bottom lip came out like a drawer. But Mr Boyter pulled my dad aside and said something in his ear. My dad nodded and Mr Boyter said to me, 'It's OK – you're nine years old! What age are you?'

I looked at my Dad to see if it was all right to tell a lie. He nodded.

'I'm nine,' I said. 'My name's Ken Buchanan and I'm nine.'

'Well then Ken Buchanan – nine – you are in!' Mr Boyter said, and he and my dad laughed. Boy was I happy. My dad told me later that Mr Boyter had seen the disappointment on my face and couldn't turn me away.

I wanted to be in the ring so much. But my dad said to bide my time. Build up to it slowly. Learn the trade before you go in with the tradesmen. And I did. And I trained and trained, getting ready for my first contest in a couple of weeks' time. And when it came it was like getting all my Christmas presents at the same time.

Within a few weeks of joining the Sparta the club had its own championships. I was one of four in the lightest weight division: the three-and-a-half-stone class. My wee heart was beating like a train. Here it comes – my first contest. The boxing started just after five o'clock. At the weigh-in I was three stone two pounds. I remember years later that Ali told me he had lost more than that before a fight. I won my two fights that night and was club champion at that weight. I had a taste for victory. I still have the medal. In some ways it means more to me than some of the other trophies I have won. It always reminds me of my dad and Mr Boyter colluding to get me into the Sparta.

Some of the laddies would train like demons up to their first fight, but they would never come back afterwards. It would probably have been too much for them. Not just the fight and the punishment they would have to take. The whole thing – the pressure, they call it stress these days – would be too much for them. They would be among the best prospects in the club – they might even win the fight – but you would never see them again. Boxers fight because it's been in their blood from the start. That is the difference. Since eight years old all I ever wanted to do was box. Once I started boxing my ambitions changed. I didn't want just to be a boxer. I wanted to be the best boxer in the world. My heart was set on that ambition.

All the older boxers in the club seemed like giants, towering above me and snorting as they laid into the hook and jab pads or the heavy bag. And if I was impressed by the images on the Joe Louis film, this was something else. This was the real thing. The smell – that was it – the smell of leather and sweat. The sound of big hooks on the heavy bags. The steady rhythm of skipping and the speedball. Trainers shouting instructions to fighters in the ring. It was all there. And me? I soaked it all up. In through my eyes, my nose, my ears. And my hands. I punched the heavy bag. It never moved. It just hung there as if it was made of stone, like a pillar holding up the building. Probably the older boxers had a wry laugh at my antics that first night. But boxers are quick to take you under their wing and show you the ropes, if you'll excuse the pun, especially if they see you're keen. And, boy, was I keen. I was right in there, head down raring to go. Early to arrive for training and last to leave. I lived boxing. I bought the magazines, the books. Studied it like a science. And my dad caught the bug too, because he came along with me to the gym every night.

When we got home I'd study various punches with my dad. He'd put a pair of boxing-gloves on and kneel down to my size. I'd practise single punches and some combinations. *Jab – jab – cross – jab cross hook jab jab*. Those were the words that rang in my ears as I went through session after session of combinations. I know it sounds daft but those words are like poetry to me now, especially if I imagine it's my dad saying them. I must've looked pretty absurd with big twelve-ounce gloves on and me weighing only three or four stone.

When it got out at school that I was attending boxing club, I was never short of opponents. I was in scraps almost every week, but I was able to hold my own no matter how big and heavy they were. Even at that age I knew the man – or boy – on the street doesn't know how to throw a punch correctly. And because hardly anybody can throw one, few have felt a real punch on the chin, so when they do, they back off. There is nothing like a right crack on the beak to let you know the world is a real place. The first thing that happens is your eyes water so much you can't see, then this pain rushes through your nose and blood starts seeping down your chin. Once you're like that you're an easy target. That reaction disappears after a while in boxing, but not for the man on the street. He can look forward to that every time he catches a punch on the nose. It's all about giving and taking, and if you can't take then forget it.

One night my granny, Sarah, asked me if I wanted to go up to the Music Hall in George Street to watch the Scottish championships. Did I want to go to the boxing? The championships were always at the end of the year, so people had their big heavy coats on as we walked up the street.

There was a long queue; boxing was a bigger thing in those days. I know it's high profile now on the telly and such like, but then the ordinary man and woman on the street would go to boxing shows. Like the bingo – only with more men there. The shows were nearly always mobbed. Now people just sit in their living-rooms and watch it on the telly. It took ages to get in the main doors as the crowd shuffled along bit by bit. My gran was one who liked to save money. She wasn't mean – not to her family – but if she could avoid giving money to the big boys she did. She wasn't going to spend extra at this boxing show if she didn't need to. She had a plan to get me in for nothing. So she told me what to do when we got to the ticket booth. When we approached the ticket desk I slid up the back of her coat and put my arms round her waist. I held on tight and shuffled along with her to the ticket desk. My legs were twisted round hers and my feet resting on top of hers. I could hear some of the other people in the queue laughing. She just paid for herself and moved off.

Once we got through the main doors of the music hall, she shuffled up to this pillar. Once behind it, we were out of sight of the man in the ticket office, not that he was looking anyway. And he probably would have just laughed if he saw what we were up to. She gave the all clear and I came out from under her coat, and we both laughed. A couple of punters laughed when they saw what we'd done. It was great. She loved it as much as me, my granny. We hightailed it upstairs and watched the boxing. I mind coming into the main area and all the people milling about getting into seats and the ring lit up. It was breathtaking. The same thing you get when you're up the Highlands and you come across this bit of stunning landscape all of a sudden. She said to me: 'You'll be boxing up there some day soon.' No wonder we often thought she had second sight. We did this only once when we went to the boxing. And the thing is

– people must have seen us. They did see us in fact – because they would be laughing.

I battered on at the boxing. I was always learning – always getting better. I suppose I must have been obsessed by it. But there is nothing wrong with that – other boys were obsessed with football. I looked forwards to the day I'd be up there in the ring with people chanting my name. Just the same way other boys would imagine scoring the winning goal in a cup final. Or even for their local team.

Birthdays are a special time for everyone, but they are very special for a kid. I remember on my ninth birthday I had a realisation of how my life was to go in the immediate future. I had been going to the Sparta boxing club twice a week and was getting better all the time. Boxing's like anything else – you can make amazing improvements in the first six months, then you have to work harder and harder for each improvement after that. But I remember standing in the yard after the football. There had been no arguments that day but I'd seen three other boys looking over at me. I knew by the look in their eyes they meant trouble. Nothing happened because the bell rang. And as the bell reverberated in my head this thought came to me. I knew from that point on that I was going to be a target for other boys at my school, Towerbank. I even thought ahead and realised that I would also be a target for the older boys when I got to my next school, which was to be Portobello secondary. And my premonition – or insight, or whatever you want to call it – was right.

I kept going at the boxing and the longer I went the fewer fights I got into at school. Eventually nobody wanted to fight me. The boys at school were beginning to see me as Ken the boxer. I'd left the bible far behind now. Even my own family had started to see me as a boxer. I suppose you could say that in a lot of ways boxing made me grow up before my time. It sort of took my childhood or, more accurately, I gave my childhood to it. Everybody knew I loved anything to do with boxing.

When I graduated from Towerbank primary school to Portobello secondary I played rugby for the next three years till I left. I was the captain and stand-off for the second team of my year. I was playing rugby in the morning and football in the afternoon on a Saturday. On top of all that, I trained at the Sparta three nights a week. I have always been fit. When you are young, you don't notice how fit you are. You can imagine that whatever I played I always made sure I was in top condition. My rugby and football games were in and around Edinburgh while some of my boxing matches were in Glasgow, Dundee, Fife, Prestonpans, Bonnyrigg and several other towns outside Edinburgh. So I did have a lot of travelling to do. Sometimes I would come home from school at about four, stuff some grub in my face and get picked up to travel far away to some boxing match. The next morning I would be out on the road running and then to school – or not. I never knew another pupil who had such a busy diary.

If I wasn't doing badly enough at school already – my schooling suffered the more I became involved with boxing. If I wasn't boxing, I was thinking boxing. Other kids were doing well at school and going on to higher education. Some would eventually go on to become doctors or lawyers. But it didn't bother me. I never once was jealous or envious of them. My ambition was fixed in my head and I think many of my class knew that. As I look back, I wonder how many of those classmates reached a peak like mine in their lives? I done things beyond my wildest dreams. I began travelling the world from the age of seventeen, at a time when people from my background had not yet discovered the Mediterranean as a holiday destination. Portobello, my home town, or Troon or Saltcoats were where people went for their holidays. I boxed in the European championships in Moscow, so saw Red Square and what life was like on the other side of the

Iron Curtain – things other people heard about only on the news. Much of it is a blur to me now, except the odd crisp story that comes up now and then and re-tells itself in my head.

Over the years, my mum and dad came to all of my contests. They encouraged me every step of the way just as if I was studying to be a doctor. At boxing shows people used to shout advice into the ring. It was pretty normal and you never took much notice of it. Boxing shows were much more of a free-for-all in those days, a night out. You can't imagine some of the ear bashings I took. You could hear my mum a mile away. She was one of the most fervent shouters at the shows. She had to be the one shouting advice when the whole place was silent – engrossed in the fight.

'He's dropping his left Ken, in over the top Ken,' she'd yell. People just got used to her. *Oh that's Ken's mum!* They would say. It was a right laugh. Half the time I never heard her. You hardly hear a thing when you're in the ring, because you're concentrating on not getting your block knocked off.

I remember one contest at the Leith Victoria boxing club. I'd not done too well in the first round. I'd not used my jab enough. It was just into the second round when I heard my mum shout: 'Come on Ken – left – left!'

When she finished shouting this bloke called out, 'Come on Ken – do as yer maw's telling ye!' The whole place burst out laughing. Even my opponent smiled at me and nodded when he was ready to start fighting again. Out the side of my eye I could see the referee smiling. I can't remember how that fight went but I'll never forget all the smiles that flashed round the place. All because of my mum.

By the time I was fourteen I had been boxing seriously for six years and doing well. If you think about it, in six years a school leaver can become a doctor. But there was me at fourteen and I suppose I must have been a fairly skilled young boxer. I had to get up in the morning and do at least four miles roadwork three days a week. By the time I got back from running, my dad and my mum had usually gone to work and my wee brother Alan was off with his pals to my old primary school, Towerbank. After a bath I'd think what's the point in going to school so that some teacher can have a go at me with a belt. And even if there were no belts at schools I don't think I would have gone. Even wild horses couldn't have dragged me to school. I was home and wanted to roam and be free. The hardest part about those runs in the morning was getting out of a warm bed. Once out you were more awake than most people shuffling to work or school. It made me feel good inside, knowing that looking after my body would help me for what lay ahead.

At weekends, after my run, my mum would go outside with her fag. She would smoke it outside so that I wouldn't get the smoke up my nose. Looking back – I was pretty dedicated even as a fourteen year old. I guess if some of my pals had adopted the same attitude they may have become top football players. Nobody's an overnight success. The telly makes it look as if they are: pop stars, boxers, footballers, actors. I bet if you asked those guys you'd find they've been at it and dedicated for years and years. The thing with me was – I never knew how dedicated I was at that age. I just done what I thought had to be done. It's only looking back now I can see the work that I put in as a boy built the foundations for my success as a man.

At that age my mum knew exactly what I wanted for breakfast – I always had porridge with salt in the morning. And dinner was a high-protein meal – either eggs, spaghetti, mince and tatties or a stew or casserole.

In between these meals I would drink plenty of water and have a light snack of, say, toast and cheese or beans. But the beans gave me wind so I would go light on them. It's funny how mums seem to know exactly what you want. She knew me inside out, my mum. She even knew how I felt about the future.

School was all right. I enjoyed the gym and the only other

subject I liked was the bible class. A bit strange since you couldn't get anything so far removed from boxing if you tried. There was no flower-arranging classes! It's a strange but true fact – the only two compulsory classes, even today, in Scottish education are PE and RE. My two favourites. It's a wonder all Scottish pupils don't turn out to be lightweight boxers!

Near where I lived was the Figgate Burn Park. Growing up right next to it, I played football and cricket. I would swing from the trees and jump the burn. That required a bit of precision – you had to swing out and let go of the rope at exactly the right moment, otherwise you would crash down into the burn. When the swing seemed to stop for that second before it returns, that's when you let go. Some of the boys fell in not because they were inaccurate, but because of fear. Fear would not allow them to let go of the rope and when they eventually persuaded their hands to release their grip, they were on their way back over the burn and – splash – in they would go. Once we knew they weren't that badly hurt we'd fall about the place laughing.

At my secondary school whatever teacher was in charge that day would have each individual class in straight lines when the bell went. They were obsessed by it. They would walk up and down inspecting the line and pushing elbows and bags in so that the whole thing looked like a military exercise. So, when the bell started ringing, everybody dashed to make a line. If the bell stopped and you were not in your line you had to stand at the front and wait till everybody had gone into the school. Then the teacher would take us to his room and belt us for being late. It was like they were collecting kids to belt every day. Nothing to do with straight lines.

One morning I'll never forget was when I was late. The teacher in charge took the nautical class. The thing about him was he bent you over a desk and belted your arse with your jacket lifted up. I thought this was a bit kinky and so did other pupils. Bending young boys over a desk – and whacking them on the arse with a big strip of leather? Imagine trying that one these days? You'd be surrounded by social workers. We were all lined up in his office and he was whacking each boy in turn with his belt. It looked sore so I started thinking of a way out of it. So when he came to me I told him I had heatspots on my bum. So here's me thinking I'll get let off but he just asked me to hold out my hands.

I had forgot I had hands; I held them out in front of me. They looked funny, like two condemned prisoners saying their last goodbyes. The teacher whacked me hard three times on the hands. The first one made me wish I had just let him belt my arse. My hands went red – then purple – then they blew up like washing-up gloves. They were still swollen when the school got out at three thirty. So much for me and my great ideas. The whole school knew that he soaked his belt in vinegar to make the leather hard. Soaked in vinegar or not – you would be sore.

When I left my secondary school it took me about three weeks to find a job. It was fairly easy to get a job in them days. You never even thought about unemployment, never mind considered it as an option. I got a start as an apprentice carpenter – that's the posh name for a joiner – with a company in Rose Street in Edinburgh. Suddenly I felt like an adult. I wasn't – but I felt like one. With the boxing going well and me setting out in the world of work – everything was great. The future was looking bright. I enjoyed being a joiner and I still do. The smell of new-cut wood especially. For the first couple of years I mostly worked on windows and doors. The head joiner would be planing the bottom or side so the door or window would fit. I liked his precision and the care he took over the job, running his hand along the edge to feel the smoothness of the wood. Being a joiner is as much about touch as it is about sight.

amateur days

The Sparta boxing club was founded in the late forties by a group of Edinburgh business people. Sparta had been considered one of the best boxing clubs in Edinburgh. It is associated with many names who are familiar to fight fans all over Scotland and Britain: Bobby Neil, Bobby Horne, Jimmy Malcolm, Bertie Dunn. I could go on and on; it was a big club if you measured its success. It was also a big club if you counted the number of boys who went there. There were that many boys that they held their own club championships. And when they held the yearly contest the place was crowded to the roof. It was a big event for locals, for boxers and for the public all over Edinburgh.

From 1953, I boxed in clubs all over the country. That, I suppose, was my apprenticeship in travelling as well as boxing. Learning the trade, as my dad said. What I done in Scotland as a boy I was to do in the world as a professional. There were two rival clubs to the Sparta in Edinburgh at the time: Leith Victoria and the Buccleuch. My biggest rival and hardest opponent was from Buccleuch: Billy Appleby. But Billy had another name, they called him Tea Ticket. Why? At most tournaments there was a tea put on, usually tea and lemonade, pies and some cakes, reserved for the boxers, trainers and committee. But everybody and anybody would try to get in on it to get a free tea. Billy Appleby – Tea Ticket – was always able to get hold of more tea tickets than anybody else. Every time you saw him after a fight or a tournament he'd be stuffing his face with pies and cakes. People would queue up to get tickets off him to get into the tea. 'Has anybody seen Tea Ticket?' was the question you heard most coming towards the end of a show.

People would go out of their way to ride on the bus beside him. And people would also go out of their way to see Billy and me fight. It was always a cracker. We might have had the odd tea together, but in the ring there was no love lost between us. We both went at it hammer and tongs. And sometimes some strange situations would crop up. Like this one. Boxers have been disqualified for nutting their opponents, and they have also been disqualified for striking other boxers in the nuts. But Billy Appleby has the dubious record of being the only fighter ever to be disqualified for nutting another boxer on the nuts. Hard to believe, but it's true. It happened during a contest in the Sparta. How do I know? I was that other boxer.

It happened in the third round. Billy and me had thrown loads of leather at each other. There was nothing in the fight, nothing at all. We were both fast and clever boxers. Billy, who was a southpaw, threw a straight right hand out at my chin. I leaned back to avoid it, but my timing was out and Billy touched the end of my chin, knocking me off balance. I started to go backwards. And Billy had committed himself with the punch. His body kept coming forwards. He toppled on to me. It was like his feet and my feet were hinged to the floor. The weight of his body coming forward pushed me back on to the canvas. Crunch! If I thought hitting my head on the canvas was sore, I had another think coming. As the back of my head hit the canvas, Billy's head crashed on to my nuts.

'Jesus Christ, ma baws!!!' I shouts.

We didn't wear protectors then – or gum-shields – and I was in agony. Billy was up there protesting his innocence. 'I didn't mean it – I didn't mean it!'

It was obvious he didn't mean it. We were only about twelve

years old. You'd need to be a pair of acrobats to do that trick. His pleas made no difference. The referee awarded me the decision and Billy was none too pleased. There's the referee holding my arm up in the air. But he's got to tug it because I'm bent over like a half-shut knife. As I got up I looked over and there was Billy. He's upright looking the way a winner should – only his face is tripping him. Billy never meant it – the best thing that referee could have done was to award a draw or at least make it a no contest. We were only two young boys and disappointment is hard to take, especially when you've given as much as you have taken. Sorry, Billy.

Over the years I boxed at junior level then on to youth level and finally senior. I felt as if I had made it then. A senior boxer – it sounded good. But I still had a long way to go, a long, long way.

My very first international came in 1963 when I was only seventeen. It was against Switzerland and the Kelvin Hall in Glasgow was the venue. I was nervous, which was normal. Not so much about my opponent, but the pressure of boxing for my country, Scotland, for the first time as a senior. My opponent for that fight was Hans Aeschlimann. I stopped him in the second round. Boy was that a relief. When I went to work the next day the boys congratulated me on winning, but I just got on with the business of cutting and measuring and planing. There was something easy and simple about them days. Something that I'll never get back, I suppose.

I hoped to win the Scottish ABA championship but was beaten by Jim McMahon. It's a weird thing being a boxer. If you win, it's all smiles and happiness. If you lose, it's all doom and gloom. No wonder so many boxers end up a bit on the crazy side. Me excluded of course! Fairly soon after Jim turned professional. I remember being in awe of him. A professional – that is where my sights had always been set, of course, but it still seemed so far away. But Jim had done me a bit of a favour. By stepping down – or up as it was for him – he left the door open for me to be Scotland's first choice for amateur internationals. That year the European championships were being held in Moscow, and I was going. One thing was certain, no matter what happened I was going to do my best for Scotland, for Edinburgh and for Portobello. I must say thank you to the Scottish Amateur Boxing Association for giving me the opportunity to be present at such a prestigious event. I hope I repaid their faith in me by my effort and my behaviour.

I was still only seventeen at the time. A lot of people told my dad that I was too young to box at that level, and that he should refuse to let me go. In the Soviet Union they did not let a boxer fight at senior level until they were nineteen years old. My dad discussed this with me, but he knew how desperate I was to go. He told me that by the time I got back, I would have a better idea of how good I was. And he was proved right.

It was my first time on a plane. Sitting next to me was my pal Bobby Mallin, who was a great wee boxer and also experiencing his first fight. Dick McTaggart — he had been on hundreds of planes — leaned over and asked Bobby to wind the window down because it was getting too hot in the plane. Bobby was at the window pulling at this flap and that flap trying to get it down. Dick McTaggart was laughing with a few others behind us. Bobby eventually asked the stewardess to wind the window down because he couldn't find the lever. She sent another two steward-esses along to ask him what he wanted. They held their laughter in and told him you're not allowed to wind the windows down while the plane is in the air. By this time Dick McTaggart and his friends are pissing themselves laughing. It was a great adventure for young boys to be on, so even this embarrassment could be ignored.

As I was the youngest boxer at the championships, my fight had the honour of being the first one on. I was drawn against an Italian boxer who had won the silver medal at the previous championships. What a draw! Some people feared for my safety, and my dad later told me that had he been in Moscow with me he would have withdrawn me when he saw who I was to fight. However, I came to no harm and lost on points on a majority verdict.

For in Russia we were up against the best. And I mean the best. It was a different level, and I felt it. But I went to every show, watched every boxer closely. I spent a lot of time in the gyms with the other boxers, talking to them, asking them how they trained, how they ate. I tried to learn from them by studying their techniques and picking up as much experience as I could. And I must say they were all really helpful. Every little bit counts. But at least I had had the experience of going there. I knew within myself that I was only going to get better. I was always focused on becoming a better boxer than I already was. I was learning the trade.

There was one other great story from that trip. In 1963, times were hard in the Soviet Union so I sold all my clothes and shoes to spivs. They would come to our hotel and I would sneak them up to the bedroom. Dick McTaggart and I closed the deal on what they were going to pay us for our stuff and we thought we were getting a great deal till we started to work out how much it cost us to buy it all in Scotland. In the end we may not even have made a profit, but we had a great time spending their money at the market for presents to take back home. Funny as it may seem, a couple of us had barely a thing to wear on our journey back home.

The next year, 1964, I won the East of Scotland featherweight title. It was a great feeling to be a winner. It wiped the memory of Moscow away. I then went on to win the Scottish featherweight title – the first of my main ambitions at the time. That in turn qualified me to fight in the eliminators for my next target, the British title. In the quarter-finals against the North of England, I won. Two more fights and the title would be mine. Two more fights. I went on to the semi-finals at the Albert Hall, but it was not to be: I lost that fight in a close decision to Kenny Cooper, who was a fine boxer and one of the few gentlemen around in amateur boxing. But, as I have already said, if you learn from your mistakes and losses you gather more knowledge for the future.

I might have had a better chance if it had not been Kenny and me that met in the semi-finals. It would have been better for both of us if we had met in the final, as we were the two favourites to win that title. In the event Kenny went on to lose in the final against Ron Smith. It was a big shock, Kenny was out-and-out favourite to win that fight. But later Kenny told me that our semi-final bout had taken so much out of him that he had very little left to give in the final. He was flat and was out-boxed by the underdog. However, I did get a chance for my revenge, fighting Kenny a couple of months after that, and won. It seemed I was learning from my mistakes and gathering experience all the time.

It was Olympic year and a few boxers had already taken places in the British Olympic team. Both Kenny Cooper's club and Sparta tried to arrange a 'box off' between us and Ron Smith, so that the best man could be selected to fight in the Olympics. But Ron's club was about the most powerful club in Britain at the time so there was no way they were putting their Olympic hope up to fight anybody, whatever Ron may have wanted. As far as they were concerned they were on their way to the Olympics even if the man they were taking was not the best man for the job and so not the best man for Britain.

England had arranged to fight Italy in Rome about a month before the Olympics were due to take place. At the tournament Ron Smith was three and a half pounds overweight. He was not a true featherweight and found it really difficult to make the weight. We were told he had to sweat that extra weight off before the fight. And we all know that is not a good thing for strength and stamina.

Ron Smith should never have been chosen to represent Britain at the Tokyo Olympics. He was too heavy to be a natural featherweight, and there were two far better natural feather-weights in Britain who could make the weight. I still feel sure that Kenny Cooper or I could have done a better job for, as it was, Ron Smith was stopped in the first round of his first fight. He was again reported to be well overweight before the fight and had to sweat it off. It was one of those things – like you have in every profession: politics overruling sense. The people in the know in boxing knew that me or Kenny Cooper would have been the better choice, but there was nothing we could do about that.

Being overweight before a fight is a no-no. This sort of thing could never have happened in other countries, particularly Eastern Bloc nations like Bulgaria where the training regime is so strict. There, even if you win the country's championship, you are not automatically selected for the Olympic team. You might be fight-ing a boxer who has a fantastic record but has an off night for whatever reason when you fight him. So there would be a box-off between them to select the right one. The Bulgarians were more interested in how their country would show at the Olympics than internal squabbles and politics, so, like the Russians, made sure their best boxers represented them.

Kenny Cooper and I agreed that either one of us had a right good chance of winning a medal in Tokyo. And we were both experienced enough in boxing to look at the opposition and make a judgement like that.

For a year I got my head down and trained like a demon. Next year, at nineteen, I won the Eastern district title again. The Scottish title and the quarter-final in England followed. Now for the semi-final, where I slipped up last year. There was no way I was going to make the same mistake this year. I was going to do everything in my power to succeed this time. I won and I knew I'd stepped up a level in my ability. I knew I had reached it. Suddenly you know you are a better boxer than you were only months ago. It seems to happen all at once. You press and you train and there's nothing giving. It's like you're pressing against a wall. Then one day you find yourself on the other side of the wall. A better tradesman. I went on – finally winning the British featherweight title. You'd think I would be elated. And I was, but as soon as my hand was in the air I was thinking about turning professional. As I said – all I ever wanted to be was the best in the world. That is where I had my sights set – and that is where I was going.

In that fight I was up against Jimmy Isaac in the Royal Albert Hall. He was from a London boxing club, so he was well supported, but I had a busload of fans who came down from the Sparta to cheer me on, as well as my family. In the end, I beat him on points, and we all celebrated in style, but I wanted to savour the moment.

But I can still remember one of the last times I fought for Scotland. It was against Bulgaria in January 1965, then regarded as a very strong boxing nation. Scotland lost nine–one on our first meeting and I was the only winner from our team.

In many ways amateur boxing can sometimes be even more hectic than professional boxing, for two days later we boxed Bulgaria again. This time we lost seven–two as one of our boxers got a broken nose in his first fight and had to pull out. I won again and this time Frankie Gilfeather also came out on top. But what is most memorable about that fight is not the win but how I won, for my opponent was disqualified for biting me. He was eventually disqualified in the third round, but he had been biting me since the second. He had been clever about it, as nobody had noticed. Even my corner-man Charlie Kerr thought I was havering until he saw the teeth marks on my neck. I called him Dracula because I think vampires come from over that way – Bulgaria – Transylvania – that general area. Finally in the third round I turned round and Dracula was caught out. He was seen clinging to my neck by his teeth, growling like a dog. But I can half understand the guy. Every Bulgarian was desperate to win because they would get a chance to represent their country in the European championships later that year. The very same championships I'd

fight in. Dracula didn't want to miss that – the trip of a lifetime –
all those lovely necks to suck the blood out of.

I had won the ABA and now I had to go and fight in the
European championships in East Berlin, where I got the chance
to cross the Berlin Wall. There wasn't much more I could achieve
at amateur level now. After some thought, I decided I'd turn
professional when I got back from the Eastern Bloc.

Bobby Neil, who had belonged at one time to the Sparta, was
my initial favourite of all the managers that tried to sign me up.
There had been quite a few pursuing me since it became clear it
was only a matter of time till I turned professional because I had
been doing quite well at amateur. It excited me to know that many
good judges of boxers thought I was worth taking on. He wanted
me to come down to London before I went over to the European
championships, so I went down with my dad. When I was there
Bobby put me in the ring for three rounds with one of his boxers,
Frankie Taylor. Taylor had won a good medal at the Rome
Olympics in 1960. Thankfully Frankie did not go all-out in the
ring, but I did quite well and I thought Bobby would be
impressed. Frankie thought I had done well too.

Bobby Neil then spoke to my dad, and it was a good job he
was there. He was older and wiser and could see things coming a
mile off. He instinctively knew what would be good for me and
what wouldn't. My dad is as much part of my success as I am.
Without his guidance I don't think I would have made it through
all the potential pitfalls in the game.

In fact my dad kept a set of scales in the boot of his car, as
some of the boxers who claimed to be featherweights like me were
in fact lightweights. In these non-championship bouts, boxers
were supposed to have a weigh-in just like the professionals, but
rarely did. In fact, I do not remember seeing a set of scales at any
of these shows. My dad thought there was a lot more overmatch-
ing at amateur shows than there was at professional contests, and
he often made a point of this to the officials. He wasn't doing this

only in my interest, but for other boxers too. His complaints fell on deaf ears, and didn't make him very popular with some of the boxing offcials.

Bobby said that when I signed for him he would have to stop me dancing around the ring as much as I did, as he wanted to slow me down. This was something my dad did not agree with. It would have meant making a drastic change in my style that had brought me this far. What's more it was a style I was comfortable with, which I was developing all the time, and was the very foundation of my boxing. It seemed Bobby wanted to coach me to fight the same way as he had done. My dad told me later that, due to an accident Bobby had had in Edinburgh, he had to have a silver plate inserted in his leg and that had restricted his movement. He was going to train me to fight like a guy with a broken leg! My dad put it bluntly like he always did: 'Ken – you don't have a plate in your leg so you don't need to fight his way.'

Then, to make matters worse, Bobby said I'd need to move to London if I wanted to fight for him. That was the clincher – I didn't know anybody in London. All my friends and family were in Edinburgh. And anyway – I loved Scotland and loved Edinburgh, so why should I move? My dad told him we would get back to him. We did, with a thanks but no thanks. So that was that: goodbye Bobby Neil! I did not intend to have a stranger try to develop a new boxing style for me, as I had been doing well with the one I already had. Sorry Bobby, but even at nineteen I knew my future in boxing was to make my opponent miss me as much as possible, then counter and build up the points.

best of british

I eventually turned professional just over a month after winning the ABA, with Eddie Thomas as my manager. At the time Eddie managed Howard Winstone, a brilliant featherweight, and reigning British and European champion. It was a great place for me to learn. I sparred with Howard any chance I got. He was fast, with a lot of good moves. We must have boxed hundreds of rounds together and I learnt an awful lot from him. Thanks, Howie.

When I got news of my first professional fight, I was nervous yet at the same time eager to show the professional world what I could do. The fight was to be at the National Sporting Club at the Café Royal, Piccadilly, right in the centre of London's West End. I was up against Brian Tonks. Once I was into the first round I knew the fight was going to go my way, barring any big mistakes. I'm not boasting. There are times when after a minute with the other fighter you just know you're going to win, unless they land a big one on your chin. I ended up stopping him in two rounds when the referee stepped in and said he was unable to defend himself. That was me off to a flying start.

But I remember seeing Brian's face as the referee stepped in. He didn't know where he was, like a fish pulled from the sea. His eyes were all over the place but not recognising anything. And that helped me – that awful look in his eyes. I swore to myself I'd never get myself into that position. I wanted to go as far as I could go in boxing – the world championship was my goal – but there would be no way I'd be staying on, boxing past my sell-by date. No way at all. Once the dream started to fade, I'd give it all up for the quiet life. But for now I was going to revel in the glory of winning my first professional fight. Howie has to take much of the credit for that – all those fast rounds sparring with him paid off.

I had one fight, one win. And soon I was off. From then on in, I was fighting nearly every month and winning. It's a long, hard slog working your way up the ratings and I was impatient. But my dad and Eddie kept me focused. They could see that left to my own devices I'd be out of the blocks too fast. I was still learning the trade. I was a tradesman now but Eddie and my dad were shaping me into a craftsman. They pulled me in and made sure I climbed the ladder rung by rung. So rung by rung it went – up and up – climbing the ladder towards a shot at the British lightweight title. That's what I focused on all the way through 1966 and into 1967.

I had another four fights before the end of the year, winning them all. In 1966, I had another eleven fights which I won. I felt my career was on its way up. Already sixteen fights, sixteen wins with six KOs. I felt like a different person. I'd even met Prince Philip, the Duke of Edinburgh, in August for my fight against Ivan Whitter. He asked me if I looked at my opponent's eyes or his gloves when I was fighting. I told him I looked at his gloves. The Prince wanted to know why I didn't look at his eyes, as he had been told that boxers look at their opponent's eyes. I replied: 'I've never been whacked in the mouth with an eye before.' He laughed, I mind that, he laughed. I was training much harder and learning as I went along. I was enjoying every minute of the time whether I was doing roadwork or sparring in the gym. I completely immersed myself in boxing. On the 23 January 1967 in Glasgow I fought John McMillan (one of the many McMillan brothers) for the

Scottish lightweight title and defeated him on points. It was an exciting time for me: after seventeen wins I felt closer than ever to having a shot at the British title, held by Maurice Cullen. But I was sure that soon it was going to be mine, now that I had my first title.

Most of my fights were held in sporting clubs – big dinners and bow ties. A place where the businessman can get close to the ferocity of what it is to be in a physical fight. Close enough to taste the sweat and blood in the air – but not close enough to get hurt. It can cost quite a bit for a ticket and I have often wondered – coming from my background, where boxing was attended by your average Joe – what it's all about. The main criticism about this sort of venue from my point of view is that it's expensive and most of my fans couldn't afford it. These were the fans who had turned up to see me throughout my amateur career, and here was I repaying the hundreds who wanted to support me by fighting in a hall that priced them right out of the market. I felt like I'd betrayed them a bit. And so, I always felt I was fighting not for the fat cats in their penguin suits but for the ordinary fan sat by a telly somewhere in a pub. That's who I fought for. They had to be content to see me boxing on telly in *Fight Of The Week*. But that was the way of the slow climb up the ladder towards a title challenge. It was the way it had to be done and I hope the fans understood. I kept on going, following the instructions as to who to fight and when from Eddie and taking my training tips from my dad.

After five more wins, I was matched against the very experienced Spike McCormack. Spike could fight, there was no doubt about that. It was to be an eliminator – the winner would get a crack at the British title against Cullen. We were to fight over twelve rounds at championship weight (nine stone nine pounds) in among the suits and five-course dinners at the National Sporting Club in London.

After twenty-two straight wins I should have been

supremely confident, but I wasn't. I was nervous because this was the last stepping-stone to where I wanted to be at that time. I knew I was fit and that always gave me confidence. And I knew I had the ability and experience to beat McCormack. But this was going to be a hard fight. McCormack would want a crack at the title just as much as I did. He would believe in himself just as much as me.

Spike is much like myself, he is an upstanding boxer with a good jab and a right hand that I do not want my chin to touch. My dad got the chance to see Spike in his last fight before I met him. So we know what I am up against. Spike has far more experience than me so, rather than get too involved in the in-fighting, I stick to my left jab. By the time we have reached the twelfth and final round Spike needs a knockout to win. And by God does he turn it on. He is throwing straight jabs, right hooks, uppercuts – you name it. And as Spike is doing his stuff, I'm thinking all I have to do is keep him at arm's length. When the bell finally rang to end the fight, I think the two of us were fuckin' knackered. But the referee lifted my arm and pronounced me the winner. Fair play to Spike he says, 'Well done Ken, go get the title.' Thanks, Spike. But believe me I don't fancy too many fights like that each month; he was my hardest opponent since I turned professional.

I was so relieved to know that my next fight was for the title. But just as the rush of glory swept through me, my head started its calculating ways. I'm human and when you reach one goal another one always pops up in your head. It's like swimming towards the horizon. This time it was the Lonsdale belt all new and shining that appeared in my mind. I wanted it. But it was currently around the waist of British champion Maurice Cullen from Durham. I wonder if he was watching the fight that night. And if he was – I wonder what he was thinking. I know what I was thinking about. Him.

A couple of days into 1968 Eddie phoned with great news. I

was to get a crack at the British lightweight title. It was like Christmas and New Year all over again. Eddie had agreed for me to box Cullen in London at the Anglo American Sporting Club. The bout was set for 19 February 1968. I started calculating, it was only a matter of weeks away. I was always pretty fit because I played golf with my dad and brother Alan several times a week and had attended the gym over the New Year. All that walking gives you a good base on which to build your fitness.

But one of the main things that kept me fit was my underwater swimming. I visited the swimming baths two or three times a week. Apart from the swimming which is a great overall exercise – I used to swim underwater holding my breath for as long as I could. That might sound crazy, but it was one of the main staples of my fitness all the years I was boxing. I would recommend it to anybody interested in keeping fit. I have even heard it is a sport now – popular in Italy. The goal there is to see how long you can hold your breath underwater and how deep you can go when you're doing it. Every time they have their championships, one or two of them have to have their heart re-started. And they say boxing is a dangerous sport!

My type of underwater swimming held me in good stead when it came to boxing ten or fifteen rounds. I always had that wee bit extra to draw on – a reserve tank of oxygen. It's a big demand on the system to move around the ring as I did and throw fast and hurtful punches. You had to make sure you had the stamina. If you didn't it was like going into the desert without water. You'd be all right for a few miles and then you'd slow up and at the end you'd be at the mercy of the desert. I have always believed that underwater swimming is one of the reasons I was able to win the world title in Puerto Rico in 120°F heat. It was the hardest fight I ever fought, without exception. I have always been a believer in a boxer visiting the swimming baths at least twice a week to do the underwater swimming. Not only does it improve your lung power, it helps get the pain and tension out of your body. There's a relaxation achieved in a swimming pool that aids a quicker recovery than if you just went home and lay on the couch. You would think I had shares in the swimming baths the way I am going on here. All I am saying is – underwater swimming gives you stamina and extra breathing capacity you never thought you had. Try it!

From the minute I signed the contracts to fight Cullen in London I knew within myself I was going to take that Lonsdale Belt from him. But I also knew that to do that I was going to have to fight the best I had fought in my life. Maurice Cullen wasn't about to let his title slip away. Who would? I trained very hard for this one – every fibre in my body was focused on Cullen and one night in London. Me and him in the ring. Alone – with only our skills, strength and stamina to prove to the country who was the best man.

Soon my dad and Eddie had me down in Merthyr Tydfil – try saying that with a drink in you! They had me running up and down the steep valleys for weeks before the fight. If you have done roadwork, you will know how hard and gruelling it can be. But you get used to it until it becomes an exercise in passing time. You get so fit that it doesn't seem like exercise at all. Sometimes you're out running in the morning and you're looking at the animals and people getting up for work and you're back home before you realise where you are. Any runner will tell you that. But Merthyr Tydfil – that was a different story. It took me weeks before I reached that easy running stage. The hills were very steep. Every day was hard. And just when I thought it could not get any harder – it did.

I had good sparring from various boxers, but the best was a Glaswegian called Hughie Smith. Hughie was a light welter-weight with fast hands. And he wasn't there to make life easy for me. I had to be careful not to get caught with any stupid punches.

But I did. No boxer – no matter how good – comes off scot free doing eight rounds a night four nights a week with a useful opponent. Boy could Hughie hit you a right whack. I was beginning to look forward to London and the fight to get away from the Merthyr Tydfil hills and Hughie's left hook.

When the training finished I went up to London with Eddie and his assistant Roy Seers. Goodbye steep hills of Merthyr Tydfil. Roy took care of the medicine bag, bandages, tape, Vaseline and basically made sure nothing was left to the last minute. He organised me so that I went through the least amount of disruption possible, allowing me to focus on the fight. The weigh-in went smoothly enough. Both of us under the championship weight of 135 lbs.

When I saw Maurice Cullen for the first time, we nodded – that was all I'd usually do – but Maurice smiled and that made me feel the stronger man. It's funny how a little thing like that can tell you a lot about how a man is feeling. In this game – you should never give anything away. Many boxers get this gut feeling about a fight. An insight as to how it will end. I've heard boxers talking about it all over the world. I was no different. I felt Maurice showed too much respect for me and that is a bad thing for any boxer. OK you acknowledge some amount of respect for your opponent. But you have to be firm about who is going to be boss – outside the ring and in the actual fight. Maurice's smile had betrayed him. It's hard to understand why he might have been having some reservations. Maurice had a good record and plenty of experience to go along with it. He had been in with the best and on paper I should have been just another challenger – hard, with a good record, yes – but another challenger just the same. Maurice had the wrong attitude. But he seemed shy and out of the picture. Like he was a spectator. To me he had given up his title before the fight. But all those things are easy to say now so long after it. The main thing was that I was there to win.

I was only twenty-two with twenty-three professional wins under my belt. I was possibly a bit cocky. Hell – I *was* a bit cocky – but that is all part of the boxing game. All part of being a boxer – you have to accept boxers for that. Cockiness in boxing is a positive attribute. Yes, I was nervous. But I was sure as hell not going to show Maurice I was nervous. I won the weighing up at the weigh-in – and nobody even noticed except me and my opponent. Both of us knew that would give me the edge in the fight.

When the bell went for the first round I moved over to Maurice and began showering punches on him. I kept going trying to score as much as possible before he started hitting back. Then I was going to move and jab – move and jab. But I kept throwing the punches in and he was coming back with almost nothing in reply. I don't know how long it went on for but it seemed like thirty seconds to a minute. And that is a long time in a fight. Try laying into a bag and time it for thirty seconds. It's a good lesson in what time is. It was like he was asking me to take any shots I wanted. Eventually he came at me with some combinations and I moved and jabbed.

As the rounds progressed I was to prove the faster puncher. I was the aggressor. I was there to take what was mine. A trophy I had lodged in my mind since the Joe Louis movie, and those bouts with my cousin Robert in the back garden. Maurice knew I was there to take the title. His confidence was dented, fading with every round, because I was coming forwards and scoring he back-pedalled most of the fight. I put him on the canvas several times with fairly fast but accurate punches. Not jaw-breaking knockout blows by any manner of means. Just ones that hurt a little. Punches that said I was here to stay.

The night before the fight I had a dream. I seen me knocking Maurice out in the twelfth. It was after a flurry of punches and I caught him with this dream of a right which caught him on the chin.

But here we were in reality, in the eleventh round. Maurice had been down several times. I was feeling strong as an ox. My whole body was at optimum temperature and flexibility. I felt invincible. I could see in Maurice's eyes that he was looking tired and hurt. I decided to go for it. Turn up the pressure. I stepped in with some jabs and then moved up to combinations. He kept going backwards – slipping some of the punches but taking a lot of punishment. I pummelled him from corner to corner. Then, just a few feet from his corner, I caught him with an array of head punches. Every one of them connected. And there's always a slight delay between a good punch landing and the corresponding reaction in your opponent. His knees buckled first and then Maurice dropped to the deck. It was the third last or fourth last punch that done it.

It was slow motion watching him try to get back up. He looked at me – then the ref. His eyes were a little bleary. I am saying to myself, stay down – stay down. I wanted it to be over. For me to be the champion. The referee was counting away there. *One, two* – he couldn't have counted any slower as far as I was concerned. *Three, four, five*. Maurice is on his knees. Oh shit, if he gets back up I'll have to do it all again. That's what I am thinking. *Six, seven*. I am pressing in there hoping he stays down but ready to go for it if he gets back up. I am certain it's going to go the distance. The adrenaline is rising in me again and I am prepared to go that extra mile to win. *Eight, nine* – and Maurice is on his feet and straightened up. The referee has got his gloves in his hands and is turning them as if by doing that he'll be able to tell something about the man. I never understood why referees do that. But I can see from away in the a neutral corner that Maurice has lost the will to go on. My dad was leaning into the ring. The whole place was silent. The referee is looking in Cullen's eyes as he says *Ten* and waves the fight over.

Yee Haa!!! I was British champion in my twenty-fourth outing. I jumped up. I was up in the air for what seemed like half an hour.

The whole place – well, my fans anyway – was rising up out their seats. My dad was halfway into the ring. I landed on the canvas British champion! Ken Buchanan – British champion. I could not believe it. I think I cried but I can't remember right – it was such a powerful moment in my life. How many of them that went to school with me had ever felt like this? That sort of experience is only given out to very few. No wonder it is so difficult to get. I looked over at my dad. The whole world shrunk to me and him. All the noise disappeared – it was just my breath and my dad with his big smile and his outstretched arms coming at me through the throng of people who were now in the ring. How must he have been thinking? Here was his son. A stick insect at eight – skin an' bone – three and a half stone at his first fight – here he was winning the British title. A boy, an ordinary boy from Portobello. The rest of the crowd could have been doing the hokey cokey and we wouldn't have noticed. My dad reached me and hugged me. 'Your mum'll be really proud of you son,' he said. 'And so am I.'

I don't know if there were tears in his eyes, but there were tears in mine. Tears – when I had never felt better in my life. It's a strange thing – life. It was going to take something to beat this. Something big. And then in the midst of all that energy it came again – that point where we change our goals. I had hardly become the British champion and already I was thinking about the world title. Bring on the world was what was going through my mind. Bring on the world – could I be world champion one day? Me?

I fought another nine times while holding the British title, but the shine was going out of these fights. Soon no serious contenders would fight me and I couldn't see a way forward to the world title that I wanted. I needed something else. I needed something bigger and better: a challenge. I started to lose all my motivation, and went into retirement totally disillusioned with boxing. I took up my trade as a joiner once more.

I remember how boxing had looked like a right hard life for

very little reward. Up at six in the morning then off to the gym in the evening. No parties, no dancing and having to sleep in the spare bedroom three weeks before the fights. And for what? For about one and a half grand a year – that's what. It's hard explaining to people about the money. They think if you're a high-class boxer – British title holder, say – that you must have earned hundreds of thousands, if not millions. It's one of those things – if you've been on the telly you must be loaded. It's all nonsense. Like every other walk of life, the people at the very top of the tree are making the money and everybody else is trying, or struggling, to make a living. I was getting one and a half grand a year at the time I was British champion. Why? Well – one of the reasons was I couldn't get any big fights. I held that title for almost two and a half years as I couldn't get any challengers. I defended it only once in that time.

What further disillusioned me was that all my fights took place in clubs – at boxing dinners. There was never any money in these fights. I went on a complete downer with the whole boxing world. So I returned my Lonsdale Belt to the British Boxing Board of Control and asked them to cancel my contract with Eddie Thomas.

It was right about this time that tragedy struck. My mum, Cathy, died. I personally think that as you come from your mother there is this built-in bond which only a mum and her son or daughter have. My mum always came to my boxing shows and she always got on well with any other mums who were at the shows. I loved my mum more than words can say and when she was taken at the age of fifty-one I was devastated. It was eleven months before I won the world championship. It has and still does bother me. A man can say he misses his mum. He's all the more a man for that.

When I said there is some kind of bond between a mum and child, it made me think. On the day my mum was buried my manager Eddie Thomas had come up to the cemetery. I shook Eddie's hand and told him I wanted to be the lightweight champion of the world. It would have been what she wanted – she was proud I'd made it to British champion, but the world title would have meant so much. I told him I wanted to be champion so that when I visit my mum's grave I can show her my world championship belt. At the funeral the memories came flooding back. I could thank her for all the mornings she stood in the coal shed smoking so that the smoke wouldn't go up my nose while I was having the breakfast she prepared and getting ready for school. And I remembered how she supported me throughout my amateur career, shouting instructions from the ringside.

It has been hard getting over mum's death, and I suppose I never will get over it. I hardly spoke about it then, and I hardly speak about it now. My dad was never one to push me on anything I did not want to do. Nor did he push me into speaking about things I didn't want to speak about. But I must say, as the years went by, he helped me tremendously when I needed to speak about boxing or my mum.

My mum dying made me come out of retirement. I wanted to win a world title and I was going to do it for her. I was hoping to conquer the world. But there's another ladder there too. Just as they had done with the British title my Dad and Eddie were teaching me patience on the world scene. By the inch it is a cinch – but by the yard it is hard. I was desperate to move up in the world ranking. Get close to that place where you're hovering about eliminators for the world title. But there was somebody who was standing in my way. There was always somebody standing in the way. This time it was a Spaniard called Pedro Carrasco. Carrasco was the reigning European champion. I wanted to fight him but before anything could be done he stepped up to light welterweight. The title he held was up for grabs. I was over the moon when the British Boxing Board of Control put my name forward as a challenger. It was ironic but

Spain had another equally good prospect in Miguel Velazquez. The scene was set for me to travel to Madrid and fight Velazquez for the vacant European lightweight title. The fight would be on 29 January 1970.

blue laguna

I trained like I always did: hard and dedicated. I was in great condition when Eddie, my dad and me flew to Spain the morning of the day before the fight. You'd think that would bother me. Arriving in a country a matter of hours before the fight – but when you're confident that you've done all you can in your training then nothing should be a problem. Probably if you had doubts about your own fitness you would let little things worry you. Once there is a crack in your confidence, there are a hundred wedges waiting to go in there.

I was blessed with one of those bodies that never puts on weight. I never had a problem making nine stone nine. So on the afternoon in Madrid – like most boxers – I want to know what my weight is. I am not worried in case I don't make the weight. It is much simpler than that. I want to know what I can eat and drink before the weigh-in the following day.

Eddie had arranged to have a set of scales in my hotel room. I undressed and jumped on – still talking to my dad about the ins and outs of the fight. The only thing on my mind was how much I'd be under and so how much grub I could safely scoff. Shit! I was three pounds over the weight.

Eddie checked the scales and said they were OK. What the hell was I going to do? I had never been over the weight before. Never! It was a blow, a big psychological blow. And to make things worse, I didn't bring any training gear. Why should I when

I never had any trouble making the weight? I never suspected for a minute I might have been overweight. I was a natural light-weight and I looked after myself. Eddie then took me to a sauna for an hour. I figured that I could sweat off at least a pound and go to bed and rest up. Sometimes you lose weight while you're sleeping – ever noticed that? How light you are in the morning compared to when you went to bed the night before?

Time was running out for me as I got to the sauna. The blast of heat nearly knocked me out as I opened the door. Luckily there was nobody else in there. It was bloody hot and the last place I wanted to be the night before a European title fight, but it had to be done. I could hardly breathe. My lips and nostrils were burning when I tried to take in a breath. I started up on the top benches but had to move down – that kind of heat just doesn't go well with Scottish lungs. But one good thing was – the sweat was pouring out of me. I must have lost a pound in the first few seconds. Aye! I wish! When I eventually came out of the sauna I felt – and probably looked – like a skinned rabbit dipped in oil. More like an old-age pensioner than a boxer about to go into a European title fight.

That night I sat in my room playing cards with my dad, something we always did. It helped me relax, and boy did I need to ease up. I was choking for a drink of water but Dad was keeping an eye on me. I wouldn't have drunk anything anyway. I had to make the weight. All night long with nothing to eat or drink. I can't remember who won at cards – but I do remember waking up in the morning with a mouth like a badger's arse. First thing I did was jump on the scales. Thank fuck! I was half a pound under the weight now. I had a glass of water. Took it sip by sip. Swilling it round in my dry mouth and swallowing every mouthful. It was the best drink of water I think I've ever had.

Everybody was there at the weigh-in. It was mobbed. The press, punters, managers and trainers. All I kept hoping was that the half a pound under was right. *I hope I'm not over – I hope I'm not over*, was running through my mind. I stepped on to the scales. I could hardly look. They slid the weights about – tap tap – it seemed to take forever. The guy shouted the weight out in Spanish. What good was that to me? But there was very little reaction so I assumed it was OK. I was just breathing a sigh of relief when Eddie shouted out that I was three pounds under. I could see Eddie making his way to the back of the crowd. As soon as I was finished I was out of there like a whippet. I was so mad I wanted to throttle Eddie, but at the same time I was relieved. The scales in the room were wrong. Eddie said he had checked them? That will be right – I wouldn't let Eddie so much as check my electricity meter since that day. At least I could have something to eat – and drink some water. It didn't matter anyway – the weigh-in was over and that was that. I was happy I had made the weight. But I felt drained and the fight was over fifteen rounds. That night I never said much to Eddie or my dad. They just seemed relieved that I had made the weight too. But it was on my mind all through the fight. Losing three pounds so quickly can't do your strength and stamina any good. I remembered Ron Smith and what happened to him in the Tokyo Olympics. *Can I go the distance?* I kept saying to myself over and over. Fifteen rounds, each three minutes.

Often I have sat on my stool waiting for the bell – tense – but not terrified. I'd be thinking *What the hell am I doing here?* But I wasn't scared of getting hurt. No, the real killer was the fear of losing. It was the worst ever because for me at this moment I had an unbeaten run of thirty-three contests. If I lost I'd have felt I had let somebody down. I don't know who. Me? My dad? My fans? Scotland? It was just the feeling that I would have let somebody down – it's hard to explain. And losing the three pounds was weighing heavily on my mind.

I did go the distance – and it was hard. I was heckled by the crowd on the way into the ring. Velazquez was declared the winner. And to be honest, even though I was drained, I thought I had done enough to win. I'd landed enough blows and stayed out of the way of enough of my opponent's blows. The British reporters around the ring thought I had won as well, but they would anyway. What I'm saying is – there are times when your pride tells you you should have won. But with passing time you realise that you lost fair and square. This fight, even with the passing of time, is one I won. I was robbed, as they keep saying in the boxing game. There are as many robbed boxers in the fight game as there are innocent men in Barlinnie Prison. Even so – this was a classic case of daylight robbery in the middle of the night.

What happened was as soon as the bell went at the end of the fifteenth round the ring was invaded by Spaniards. You never know when to expect the Spanish Inquisition. The referee turned towards my corner – looking straight at me. I was sure he was just about to announce me as the winner. The smile was already working its way across my face. But then the referee noticed there were more people in the ring than usual. He turned away from me – the crowd of Spaniards got around him. All the referee could see was crazed Spaniards. But they were not that crazy, because they pushed and manoeuvred the referee over to Velazquez. Soon I couldn't even see the referee. The crowd had him right over at my opponent's corner. And I suppose there was nothing he could do then but lift Velazquez's hand. I couldn't believe it when I saw the hand going up in the middle of the crowd. At first I thought it was some kind of joke. But it wasn't. Jack Solomons, the promoter, dashed to the referee's side of the ring, told him he represented me and tried to see his scorecard, but he couldn't get hold of it and the referee was out of the ring before you could say Dick Turpin. We even asked the promoter later but we never saw that scorecard.

Not one of the British reporters who was there thought Velazquez had won the fight. In my opinion he was not one of the better fighters I have faced in my career. If I had been Italian there was no way this fiasco would have happened. Italy at the time was a big voice in the European Boxing Commission, but Britain seemed to be no more than a squeak. We had to let it go.

Looking back now it's easy to see – and laugh – that the referee had decided the best way for him to get out of that ring alive was to award the fight to Velazquez. Hell, what would you have done? And another thing: the invasion of the Spaniards could have gone the wrong way. He might have saved my life, too, that night, who knows? Who can tell what a bunch of mad Spaniards might do next! The crowd even booed me back to my dressing-room. And – as I said – put the boot into me whenever they could. The whole thing made me sick.

After going back to my hotel room and flinging the scales off the wall a couple of times I sat on the bed thinking. Eddie and my dad left me alone to do that. Eddie especially was saying nothing because he felt himself to blame for the so-called weight problem. So where do I go now? I asked myself. I was well on my way up that ladder towards a World title and now I'd been stopped in my tracks. No way Velazquez will give me a return in a hurry now that he is the European champion. He'll hold on to that title – fight a couple of bums before taking on a true challenger. It was at this point I realised that if I was going to be the World champion I would have to fight for it. Hard! It was time to step up a gear. If I thought I was dedicated to boxing before, I was going to shock even myself now. That would mean a lot of sacrifices for both myself and my family. Sacrifices that looking back now get harder to justify, but I suppose everybody looks back on their lives much the same way. It was either that or throw all those years at boxing on the scrapheap.

I got back home. Had a couple of days off with my family and then it was back into the routine. Only this time the gas had been turned up. People on the street were still congratulating me. They thought I had done pretty well for a boy from Portobello. But it pained me to know that they thought I had gone as far as I could. They rightly thought it a great accolade that I should get to fight for a European title – and nearly win it. But that wasn't ever going to be good enough for me. No way. I dug in and trained harder than ever. In the gym, people could sense it and they've since mentioned to me that they thought I got the head down and steamed in after that defeat. I was like a man possessed. Within four weeks of my fight with Velazquez I was back in the ring, at the National Sporting Club in London. My opponent was Leonard Tavarez. I was so fit and determined that when I defeated Tavarez over ten rounds it felt like a training session. I had slipped down a few rungs on the ladder to the World title, but Tavarez was one rung back up. And I still had a bit to go even to get back to where I was before my European title defeat.

In April I went up to Nottingham and defeated Chris Fernandez from New York over ten rounds. Once again I treated it like one more rung in that ladder. I was working my way back up the rankings. I was also keeping an eye out for any up-and-coming boxers that might want to share the ladder with me. I couldn't allow that to happen. No sir. I got to hear about a useful young boxer called Brian Hudson, who was punching his way up the title ladder. My ladder. *This ladder ain't big enough for the both of us*, I thought. It was inevitable the two of us should meet. I even brought it up with Eddie. *If this kid is as good as they say then let's get on with it. I'll give him a shot at my title, 'cause he's a good contender.* After talks with Hudson's manager we signed to fight at Wembley arena on 12 May 1970. Unlike the last two fights I was apprehensive about this one. Brian Hudson was no pushover. He had an impressive amateur record winning the British light-welterweight title in 1967. I dug in again and trained hard. This was a time in my career when I seemed to be improving beyond even my own expectations. And even though I was still a very young man, I had this feeling that I was running out of time. If I was ever going to get a World title I had to get a straight run at it. And this had to be the run. I had to make sure that whoever was standing in my way – no matter how good a boxer they were – had to be beaten.

Brian Hudson was a big puncher. I had to stay out of his way, but that wasn't easy because Hudson was a boxer who liked to have a go. This was going to be a test of character for both of us.

In the third round we had a clash of heads and I came out of it with a cut over my right eye. It wasn't deliberate. Just one of those things that happens in the ring. The blood was running out of my cut and into my eye at the end of the round. My corner did the best they could with the cut and out I went for the fourth. But through this round the cut got worse. Brian kept going for it. And why not – if there's an easy way to win a fight you use it. I would be going for his cut if he had one. When I sat down at the end of the fourth, Eddie looked at the cut and said it was bad. You don't tell a boxer he has got a bad cut unless it really is bad. I asked him how bad it was. He said it would not see me through to the fifteenth round. So here I was in another important fight and defeat was staring me in the face. If I was going to win I had to do something special. There was no way I wanted to leave that arena that night feeling the same as I did in the European defeat against Velazquez. This would be worse in fact, because I'd lose my British title. What to do? I had to go for it – that's what.

That gap between the fourth and fifth rounds was the turning point in this fight. The turning point in my thinking. The moment when I knew what fighting hard meant. If I didn't win this fight then that could have been effectively the end of my career – the boxing world would take me less and less seriously. I went out for the fifth round knowing a knockout was the only way I was going to keep my title. The only way I was going to hang on to my career. The only way I was going to hang on to my dreams of winning a world title fight.

Hudson was firmly focused on my cut. I had to catch him cleanly on the chin. But as every fighter knows the harder you try to land a big one the more it eludes you. Nothing ever seems to come off when you want it to. But that night belonged to me. I had made my mind up before I came out for this round: I was going to make the sacrifices count. Me and my family were not going to suffer for nothing. All the training in Merthyr Tydfil, all the running up hills, sparring sessions in the gym, round after round of pounding boxing were not going to be wasted.

I press and press, trying for that magical punch. All the time he is catching my cut and it's getting worse. The referee keeps glancing in at the cut, on the edge of stopping the fight with every glance. The magic punch. The magic punch. Just as it seems as if it is never going to happen it is offered to me on a plate.

Brian drops his left hand slowly as if to say, *Come on hit me*. He is trying to lure me in. He must think I am tired because my punch rate has fallen. But I know that my punch rate no longer matters because there is no way this fight is going the distance. So he drops his left hand to lure me in. In his mind he is going to land his right hand on to my chin. But I am faster and before Brian can unleash his big punch I bang *him* squarely on the chin. He looks surprised as he goes down – his right hand halfway through the air stops dead on its journey to my chin. Crash – he hits the floor. I step in but the referee keeps pushing me back. I want to see his eyes. To see if he is getting back up – you can always see that in their eyes. But the referee prolongs my agony by pushing me to the side. The crowd is tense. The referee counts. But after he gets to four and Brian hasn't moved – I know. I do not jump up this time, I am just glad that I have retained my British title. My dad hugs me. I am only relieved that I am leaving that arena with my dreams still intact. And maybe another rung up the world ratings.

I took a week off, did some swimming, some golf, then got back into my training again. I was pretty fit and waiting for Eddie to arrange another fight for me – one that hopefully would get me closer to that world title fight. One night in July the phone rang. I picked it up not knowing it was going to be one of the most important telephone calls of my life. All I heard was, 'Hello, you miserable Scots git!'

It was Jack Solomons, the daddy of all the promoters in Britain. 'Hello, you miserable Scots git,' he says again. 'Listen Ken, how would you like to fight for the world lightweight title?'

'Aye right,' I says. 'Why not make it two world titles?' I thought this was some kind of wind-up that Eddie and my dad had set up for me.

Jack just repeated what he had said, only laughing more this time. 'How would you like to fight for the world lightweight title, you Scots git?'

He was serious. 'You're not kidding me Jack?' I says.

'Ken – it's me. No, I am tying up the deal with my agent in New York – Dewey Fragetta.'

Dewey Fragetta – now I knew who that was. That was it. Solomons was serious. I felt my blood rush. Adrenaline flowing. A whole new – much harder training schedule started to form in my head. And if there wasn't enough adrenaline in my veins then what Jack told me next made sure there was. Jack told me Laguna's manager, Carlos Elita, is looking for a patsy. Jack said that he could get Ken Buchanan to take the fight. They wanted to know who I was. Jack told them I was just a stand-up British boxer. The type Laguna liked. I was angry.

'A fuckin' patsy? Is that what they think of me in America? Get me the fight Jack and I'll show these people just what us Scottish patsies are like and I am not talking cow shit either.'

'OK,' says Jack. 'But the fight will be in a very hot climate. You better train in a sauna.'

'I'll train inside a fuckin' volcano – patsy! We'll see.'

'The heat over there will be to Laguna's liking not yours.'

'I am going to beat this guy if only for what they said. Patsy? I'll give them patsy.'

Jack laughed that big laugh of his at the other side of the phone. He probably meant to get me all riled up. I am not saying that Laguna's camp were not looking for a patsy. They were – but Jack knew that sort of talk would light my fuse. He knew there was a fight to be had out of this and if I won he could get in on the act. Big money – that is probably what was at the back of Jack's mind, and he was happy I accepted the fight. But none of that mattered to me. None at all. The main thing was – here was I with a crack at the world title. It was a chance a long time before I figured I would get one. I was going to do everything in my power to win that title.

'Great,' said Jack. 'I'll finalise the arrangements with Eddie. I'll get in touch with him and we can arrange the rest of the business from there, all right Kenny?'

'You bet it's all right Jack!'

A couple of days went by and I heard nothing. I was starting to think it was a dream. It was like way back when I asked my dad to take me to a boxing club and nothing happened. Then I started to think that Jack or Laguna's camp had changed their minds. Maybe they had found out that I wasn't the patsy they heard I was. I found myself wishing that they *had* heard I was a patsy! Maybe the defeat by Velazquez would come in handy after all. You never know what it's all about in life do you? I was beginning to panic that this crack at my dream was going to fall by the wayside, but then Eddie phoned. The fight was on right enough. I was elated. It was to be held in San Juan, Puerto Rico on 26 September 1970. It was going to be a big fight. The Puerto Ricans loved boxing. It would draw a massive crowd so they were holding it outdoors in a baseball arena. In order to weigh the odds further against me the fight would start at two in the afternoon. It would be hot at that time; maybe as much as 130°F. *Jesus*, I thought, *I'll die out there*.

It was at that moment I realised if I were to become the world champion then it had to be this fight, away in a country I had hardly heard of. I knew there was no promoter in Britain ready to put up money for me to have a shot at the title. I had to go for this in a big way.

I gave my dad a phone to tell him everything had been

finalised. He was delighted. But after the excitement died down he started to talk to me the way he always did before fights, straight and serious. He knew a lot about boxing and knew a lot about current boxers. My dad cautioned me that Laguna was one hell of a boxer – I would have to be at my best to step in the ring with that guy. He knew I would be – he was just letting me know that everything had to be perfect in my build-up to the fight. And another thing: he told me to stay away from Laguna in the ring. 'Do not get drawn into a fight with him. Box – because Laguna could punch. Hard.'

I guess all dads are protective of their sons. Especially in boxing where the least mistake can get you hurt. And more especially when you're boxing at world-class level, where one mistake could mean serious injury. As we spoke I kept running over in my head the time I went to that Joe Louis film with him. All those years had passed and here was I still on course to my dream of a world title shot. OK, there had been some mistakes and mishaps – but I had the ability to get back up and carry on any time I had landed on my arse. Sometimes I think that is the only difference between winners and losers, the successful and the unsuccessful in any walk of life. The winners get up off their asses, dust themselves down and carry on, learning from their mistakes. The losers stay on their asses and make excuses blaming everybody else in the world for their failure. This time I knew success was out there for the taking, and it was only me that could take it. There was nobody that could do that for me. It would be two men in the ring pitching their strength and ability against each other.

The month before I left Edinburgh I ordered a new Daimler car. I went to this shop in the west end of Princes Street. They had new Daimler Sovereigns, which were just coming on the scene at the time. I fell in love with it right away. The car was about £2,000, which was a lot of money then. The salesman asked, 'Are you going to win this fight?'

'I fuckin' better because if I don't I won't be buying this car,' I answered.

But before I even went to America I was quite confident that I was going to win that fight. I somehow realised I was going to be the new champion, that I would be able to come back and afford the car no problem. The purse for the fight was just $10,000 (around £4,000 in those days). You can see that the purse wasn't much when you compare it to how many Daimlers you could buy for a world title purse these days. I spent more than half of my purse on that car, but it was what I wanted.

I flew to New York with my dad and Eddie. It was a long flight and I kept going over my training routine to see if there was any way I could improve it. On arrival at JFK we were met by John Condon, the publicity agent for Madison Square Garden. Even though the fight was down in Puerto Rico they had their hands in it. I suppose at that time the promoters and The Gardens ran boxing at world level. I have to say that we were treated like royalty. Once we were booked into our hotel John Condon took us to our first press conference. That was my first meeting with Ismael Laguna, lightweight champion of the world. He hardly looked my way. I was a mere fly in the ointment to him, a punchbag from Scotland. I could tell he had prepared to meet a patsy. He didn't show me disrespect – he just never acknowledged me at all. Well, this was one patsy he was never going to forget.

Given the fact that this was a big fight everything went well at the press conference for the both of us. There was no slagging each other or bragging. I was surprised by how civilised the whole thing was. There was none of that macho bravado stuff. No glares or stares. Nothing for the press to latch on to.

Later that day I went sightseeing for a couple of hours round about New York. Here was the boy from Portobello, the boy who didn't have what it takes to be a lawyer or a doctor or a civil engineer, walking about the streets of New York. I felt great, and I felt confident. A world title fight coming up and I felt confident.

I couldn't remember feeling like this before. It was soon time to go back to the hotel and get organised for the gym.

The gyms in the States are amazing. It seemed like the whole world wants to be boxers. I was made very welcome. It turned out that Laguna and I were to use the same gym for training. But it was arranged that Laguna would train at five thirty. I would train at six thirty. The first thing I noticed was that Laguna was only doing an hour in the gym. I thought the world champion would be doing much longer sessions than that. The sessions I had been doing at home were much longer. It gave my confidence a little boost.

When I arrived at the gym Laguna was just finishing his sparring. That gave me the opportunity of seeing him in action. I stood about watching him. I don't even know if he knew I was there. If he did he never cracked a light. If he had turned round he'd have noticed my smile growing. As much as I was impressed by what he could do, I knew I could beat him. It was some feeling. Much more powerful than when I got the phone call from big Jack Solomons. I was watching the only thing that stood between me and my dream of becoming world champion and I knew I could beat him. But there was still something else nagging away at me. The fact that the fight was going to be in the searing heat of the Puerto Rican afternoon sun. That could sap my strength even if I had the ability to beat Laguna.

I watched Laguna till he had finished. He then went off for a shower while I changed. He never acknowledged me as he passed, but I am sure he knew I was there. I started my session with some shadow boxing then donned my gear to spar with some New York fighter. He looked like a weight-lifter compared to me. He was at least a stone heavier than I was. But he was slow and it allowed me to practise moving in with combinations and moving back to avoid his punches. After a couple of rounds I was warmed up and moving with fluidity. Laguna had dressed and came out into the gym ready to go. He walked right past me while I was sparring. I even put on a wee show for him. But he never noticed. You'd think that would bother me – being ignored by my opponent. And worse – being ignored by an opponent whose manager thinks you're a patsy. But it didn't bother me one bit. In fact I got a boost from it. Why? It seemed Laguna thought he was too good to stand around watching me spar. He was going into this fight with his winning a foregone conclusion. And any boxer will tell you that is a big mistake. Especially with Ken Buchanan – underwater swimmer – coming at you in search of his childhood dream.

I was so happy. Everything seemed to be going well. I worked my sparring partner over for about six rounds then stopped. By the end he didn't know what was happening to him. I don't know what they were paying him, but he certainly earned his money that day.

That evening we all went out for dinner and took in a Broadway show: *The Jazz Singer*. It was great sitting there in a theatre in New York watching that. And halfway through the show it struck me how much we have in common. Me and Al Jolson. People who are obsessed with what they do. They all have one thing in common. Nothing will stop them. They are focused on something and their whole life becomes a journey towards that thing. Nothing could stop Al Jolson and nothing was going to stop me. I was going home with a world title. We went home singing 'Mammy' and off to bed. In bed that night I couldn't stop thinking about my mum. Part of me was going to win this title for her. I know she would have loved to have been there. Probably shouting in the ring: *Left Ken – left – keep jabbing!*

In the morning the excitement was turning up again. We were flying to Puerto Rico in the hot, hot, hot. Laguna here I come. I couldn't wait to get in that ring. Have you ever been hit with a wave of heat? Wow! When I stepped off that plane in San Juan it was just like that sauna in our hotel in Madrid before the Velazquez fight. Only this was dry heat. I found it hard to breathe. My dream slipped away from me a little bit as we crossed the tarmac.

I found out that the temperature was around 120°F and boy was I melting. That is nearly twice as hot as what we in Scotland consider a heatwave – 70°F. Even the smallest bit of exercise made me sweat. Good Lord – walking across the tarmac made me sweat. I asked Eddie, 'How in hell am I supposed to fight in this?'

'You'll be all right on the day Ken boy,' he said, but the sweat was running out of him too.

He took a hanky out his pocket and wiped his forehead. He looked like a gangster in an American movie. The sweating South American drug dealer. The sweat was running into my eyes. And I felt like somebody had knitted me a jumper three sizes too wee and made me wear it. No matter what I did I could not get my lungs to feel filled with air. This was going to be one hard fight. Christ! It would be hard enough shadow-boxing for fifteen rounds never mind trying to hit an opponent and avoid him trying to hit you.

Sometimes fate intervenes in your life. It had in mine a couple of times and now it was about to happen again. We were approached by Bill Daly. Bill was the ex-manager of Carlos Ortis. He told us that Laguna's manager, Cain Young, was flying in a judge and a referee especially for this title fight. Bill told us of his fear that if we didn't get rid of them it would be almost impossible for me to win.

This would be especially true if it went the distance and was decided on points. And on paper this fight looked like going the full distance. Laguna would be a hard man for me to knock out. We thanked Bill and decided to act on his tip-off.

There was also something else on my mind. In late 1966 I'd met Carol in a disco in Edinburgh. We got on well, and soon love blossomed. We became engaged the following year and in June 1968 we got married, while Carol was still in her teens. We'd bought a small semi in Corstorphine, on the outskirts of Edinburgh, which was great as it meant I could do my roadwork in the fresh country air. I'd converted the garage into a small private gym so I didn't always have to go in to the Sparta. Now, with a world title fight about to happen, I couldn't forget what was going on at home: Carol was about to have our first child, Mark.

It was very hard to concentrate. I had more mixed emotions putting a strain on myself than I wanted building up to a big fight. I had to keep telling myself that I was getting a shot at the title. You have to go for it Ken I kept saying – a hundred and fifty per cent. The bairn's future is in this too. I phoned home every opportunity I got to hear if there were any reports from the front. The two biggest events of my life were converging. Fate was dealing me a strange hand. Looking back now it's easy to see that the birth of my son was the more important and meaningful thing. But a crack at the world title in them days – to me, well! So much going on outside and in my head. I had to stay level. Stay sane. Focus.

Nine days before the fight I came into La Concha Hotel after training. The receptionist told me I had a call coming in at six pm. Well – it was about five at this time. I was pacing the floor, and remember thinking this is exactly what I should be doing. Only the floor I should be pacing is thousands of miles away. In a hospital ward. Eventually, six came and the phone rang almost dead on.

I let the phone ring once and picked it up to hear Carol's mum, Anne, say, 'You have a beautiful son!'

'Oh ya fuckin' beauty!'

I don't know if the Puerto Ricans knew exactly what that meant, but they knew I had got some good news because they all started congratulating me after it – even before I told them I'd just had a baby son. Well, my wife just had a baby son. I felt the release of so much strain. I was floating in that hotel lobby like a butterfly. No man could be happier. I even forgot about the fight for a couple of minutes.

Later I went down to the hotel restaurant like I was walking on clouds. *I'm a Dad!* I told the head waiter. Could he bring over a bottle of champagne? He did, and opened it up. I had one mouthful and left my dad and Eddie to finish the bottle. Even with the dizzy news of a newborn son and a mouthful of champagne fizzing round my teeth, I know I have to get my head back on the fight.

I remember turning to my dad and saying, 'What's it like being a grandad?'

He was fifty-six at the time. 'I'm too young,' he replied.

It was great getting to the hotel and lying about for a while in the air-conditioning. I had to get up at half five in the morning when it was cool enough to do my roadwork. I loved the noise of the crickets and the tropical smells in the air as I jogged along. In Scotland it can take up to half an hour to warm up to the right temperature in roadwork. Here I was warmed up after a few moments. I was in great condition. There were times out on those roads that I felt like I could have run forever. And to tell you the truth – I have never really enjoyed running – I seen it more as part of the job. But out here – in that heat – I loved it. Once I'd warmed up, the roadwork consisted of running between palm trees down the road from the hotel. Jogging along – then short, sharp bursts of speed – then back to jogging again. In the bursts of speed I went flat out – running to my limit. My dad and me came up with that idea.

The idea for the short bursts of speed was to get my body used to boxing in spurts. We had decided that because I'd be fighting in all this heat I wouldn't be able to keep up permanent pressure on my opponent. The tactics were to avoid being hit for a while, go into attack mode for some time and revert to avoiding being hit. That way I could accumulate the points but stop Laguna building up points of his own.

The roadwork was going well. By the time six thirty arrived the sun was out. And it was blazing down. All I had on were a pair of short pants, running boots and socks. My sweaters were both soaked through with sweat. As the days progressed my dad got slightly worried that I was losing too much weight. I had arrived in Puerto Rico looking lean and fit, but now I was starting to look gaunt.

I was taking salt tablets each day but they weren't holding back the effects of the heat. The heat was immense and I ended up well under weight too soon before the fight. I was starting to get worried about it. My dad was always resourceful. He got talking to the locals and they took us to a chemist's. We spoke to this guy in there who introduced us to a rep who gave me cartons of orange powder, after showing me how to mix it up. He told me it was being used by all the top athletes in the world, long-distance runners especially. It was chemically formulated to replace the goodness in the body that you lost while training. The orange drink tasted very salty but I persevered. Every time I felt thirsty I downed some of that rather than water. I felt the benefit right away. My weight started to go back up again. By the end of the week I felt very strong. And because of the training in that heat – very, very fit. I was ready to go the full fifteen rounds if necessary. Looking back now I realise what that stuff was. It was the same as Lucozade Isotonic – that is how much sport has progressed now. The man in the street who goes to the gym twice a week is getting the same stuff out of a vending machine that was once the food of top athletes. I wonder what the top athletes are taking now? Say no more.

At the Hospitality Inn a few days before the fight my dad met up with the boxing reporter from the *Daily Mirror*, who had come from New York to cover this fight. He was the only British reporter who bothered coming down as the press in general thought that I had little or no chance of winning. Anyway, my dad discussed with him what Bill Daly had told us about the danger of a biased referee and judge. Together they spoke to the president of the Puerto Rican Boxing Commission, a Mrs Passerella. She was all ears. It was pointed out to her that when her son – who was a professional tennis player – played in Britain he always got a fair deal. She agreed. They all agreed that it would not look good for Puerto Rico if I got a raw deal.

Then my dad pointed out that, since none of the boxers was from Puerto Rico, she'd not be doing any of the local officials or referees any favours by allowing Cain Young to bring in his own. It would appear that none of her officials was capable of officiating over such a big event as a world title fight. That clinched it. And we weren't trying to pull a fast one. It actually made sense then and still makes sense today. It was the fair thing for all concerned. The two non-Puerto Rican officials who had been flown in by Cain Young were not allowed to take part in the proceedings. The bout was judged by two Puerto Ricans and one Panamanian. Man, did I sigh a sigh of relief then. I felt that my chances had just been enhanced a good bit. We certainly owed a lot to Bill Daly, and me and my dad thanked him. But I would like to say thanks again, Bill.

Bill also told us that he had warned Eddie Thomas before we even arrived in Puerto Rico, but Eddie felt it was better to leave it until he could speak to Jack Solomons. However, as Jack was not due to arrive until the day before the fight, that would almost certainly have been too late. Thinking back now, I suppose it is possible that in the back of his mind even Eddie thought I had little chance against Laguna, but it is more likely he thought there was nothing he could do about the situation.

As the fight was two o'clock in the afternoon the weigh-in was to be at seven in the morning. That would allow both boxers to eat a reasonable meal and then prepare for the fight. At the weigh-in Laguna came in just on the 135 pounds limit. I was two pounds lighter and feeling as strong as an ox, down in no short measure to the rep and his magic orange drink. I spent the rest of the morning relaxing.

Soon it was time to go to the arena and get ready. It was

always my dad's habit that when Eddie bandaged my hands he'd go into my opponent's dressing-room. He'd watch my opponent's hands being bandaged up. The reason he done this was to ensure no sticky tape was put over the knuckles. Boxers would put the sticky tape over the knuckles so as to ensure they had a harder punch. It was like getting punched in the face by somebody wearing a stookie. The rules were that the tape had to be kept to the base of the knuckles.

So, when I was being bandaged, Laguna's manager came charging in to my dressing-room to watch Eddie bandaging my hands. Eddie had almost finished bandaging them when Cain Young started shouting. He kept saying that the tape was over my knuckles. I looked – it was nowhere near them. It was where it should have been: right along the base of my knuckles. I felt that all he was doing was deliberately trying to upset me. Things were not looking good. I noticed that Cain Young had a pair of scissors in his hand. I was afraid he might try to stab Eddie. Fortunately my dad arrived back at that point. He looked at my hands and told Cain Young they were bandaged just the same as Laguna's. But Cain Young was still not convinced. He was still going on about it, but my dad settled it there and then.

'Bring Laguna in here and we'll compare hands.'

'What?'

'I said bring your boxer in here and we'll compare the tape!'

Cain Young stared at my dad. Then my dad said to bring Laguna in and we can strip all the bandages off both of us and re-do them with everybody watching. Cain Young paused then stormed out of the dressing-room. You would think that would put a stop to the nonsense. But no, there was more to come on the way to the ring.

The next loneliest place to a boxing ring must be the dressing-room before the fight. Or maybe after a fight if you're the loser. Once you're bandaged and gloved up there is a silence that sometimes falls on the place, especially when the stakes are high. And this day the stakes were higher than they'd ever been for me. As I sat there with my boxing-gloves on loose I thought of Scotland – and Edinburgh. There had been an article in one of the New York papers that morning about my home city:

> Edinburgh is the first city of Scotland, a living and growing symbol of the Scottish way of life. Like Rome, it is built on seven hills and is one of the world's most fascinating and impressive capitals. Its Castle and Museums house treasures beyond price. It brags about its scientists, artists, poets and scholars, and of course its passionate Mary Queen of Scots. The Edinburgh Castle stands regally in the center of the city between two main thoroughfares. New Yorkers may best visualize this great monument by picturing it in the heart of Times Square, except that it is abounded by the trees, flowers, lawns and monuments of Princes Street Gardens rather than by the honky-tonks, hot-dog stands and hookers of Broadway.
>
> The population of 300,000 is practically devoid of black people and funeral parlors. Its rolling green hills, the greenest of which house many fine golf courses, are protected from the winds by well-appointed trees. It is a city of little green doors behind which are old country mansions. It is a city where clothing stores offer the best of Scottish woolens on the time payment plan and the wrong side of the road is the right side. The elegance of its chimneys, centuries old, is marred by television antennas and at the Edinburgh airport women and children get preferential boarding. For the most part the Scots are a cultured people. As evidence they offer Sir Walter Scott and Robert Louis Stevenson, their libraries and galleries and their great university which is noted for its men and women of the finest caliber is exceptional.

It made me kind of homesick, but it also made me proud. Proud to be Scottish. It fuelled my determination to win this fight for my homeland. I might be thousands of miles away from Scotland but in my heart I was home. My mind raced back to when I was eight years old – three stone two pounds in weight and winning the Sparta boxing club's three stone seven pounds championship. It had been a long road. And today I was going to do it for Britain – for Scotland – for Edinburgh – for Portobello – for my family and for myself. For that wee skinny boy in the big shorts all those years ago in the Sparta.

'Come on, Ken!' shouts my dad. I wake up from my day-dreaming. The time has come. I take a big intake of breath and get my mind back on the job at hand.

'Is it still as hot out there?' I asks him.

'Naw son, there's a slight breeze blowing over the ground so I think it'll do you good,' he shouts back.

In the dressing-room the air was thick with heat. It wasn't easy to breathe, even though I'd become acclimatised a bit to the place. After jumping about and shadow-boxing a couple of minutes it was downright hard to breathe. I took another slug of the rep's magic orange drink and headed out there. Going out to the ring I was flanked by my dad and Eddie. I also had two bodyguards to stop anybody grabbing me and roughing me up. I felt like royalty. The heat was building up as we moved from the shadow into the sun. But we were wrongly directed to the ring which was out in the open. As we approached the ring I could see Laguna was already inside the ropes and standing in the shaded corner, hardly moving. He was already conserving energy and avoiding having to deal with the sun.

The dirty bastard, I said to myself. He had gone in the ring before the challenger and taken the shaded corner. The sun was beating directly down on my corner. That made me mad. But it's a madness I can control – like a pot boiling away with the lid on it. Anyway, Jack Solomons borrowed a lady's parasol to shade me in my corner. And what my dad always said was going through my mind, 'If you lose the head, you lose the fight – if you lose the head, you lose the fight.'

The pressure's building up inside me but I am going to use it and I am going to use it good. I climbed into the ring not knowing that this was going to be the hardest fight I'd ever fight inside a boxing ring.

Ding ding, the bell goes for the first round and we both meet in the middle of the ring. We touch gloves which is an order in all fights whether title fights or not. Then we get down to the job at hand. Laguna comes out and shows me what he has got. And it's a lot. He has obviously got the idea that he can finish this quick – an easy pay day. He is a fast, intelligent boxer. He can use his left jab to take your eyes out. Laguna shows me he has got all the punches in the textbook. Plus more. And a few more than that.

But I keep to the tactics me and Dad spoke about. Stay away from his punches and then go on the attack in energetic flurries. It seems to be working. And even though Laguna has a good sharp jab, I don't feel any great force behind it. It's a good job because he is catching me with it quite often. It's only round three or four when I can tell Laguna has given up on trying to knock me out or stop me early. He has settled into scoring points. He has decided that he'll go the distance and win this one on points. But he is not finding that too easy either because I am keeping well out his road. I get the feeling as the rounds go by that he has decided to save himself for a good finish. That always impresses the judges. His backing down a bit makes me all the more determined to push the fight. I take the fight to him. Pressurising him. He seems quite surprised at first. But I can tell he thinks this is only a temporary tactic by me. That in this heat I'll burn myself out in a couple of rounds. He is still treating me with no respect. And that is what will bring about his downfall. Laguna tries all the fancy moves to stop me picking him off. But he can't shake me off and you can see it is beginning to frustrate him. He tries some wild punches –

and from those I can see that he is losing his composure. But being the professional that he is, he quickly regains his skill.

After eight rounds there is nothing in it. To the surprise of all present I am giving as good as I get. And the heat is incredible. Even though the heat is burning my arse off I still feel strong. Next thing Laguna lashes out with a deadly right which I slip past my left shoulder. He has committed himself to the punch so his body continues to come forward and – bang – we have a clash of heads. My left eye bursts open. Blood is everywhere. I am worried. The fight was slowly moving towards me and now this cut. If I lose I don't want to lose on something as unlucky as a cut. I carry on with the same tactics. But the cut is worrying me – it's worrying me no end. A couple of good blows from Laguna and the referee could stop the fight. That would be my dream over. The end. I would have to go back to Scotland with nothing to show – only a few stitches, a dehydrated body and some healthy orange powder that's good to drink. (My left eye was to hamper me throughout my career. During the fights, the left eye was the one I got cut on mostly. And in sparring that was the one that took most of the punishment. I always knew that eye was a weak spot but I didn't expect it to open up in this fight.) Laguna still hasn't caught me with any big punches. I keep on going. By the twelfth round both of us are tired. Really lead-weight tired. But Laguna will not give in. He is fighting like a true champion. He now knows he has a fight on his hands and not a pay day with some patsy. And I am not for giving up either. I am bloody well sure after coming all this way I'll not be folding up. No chance. I want this title. Probably more than him.

It's the thirteenth round and I am thinking to myself, only three more rounds to go. My eye seems to be holding up. The boys in the corner have done a good job with it. There are three rounds and I have to make them my best rounds ever. *Finish strong, Ken*, I says.

I decide to change my tactics. Instead of keeping away from

Laguna and then attacking him in energetic bursts, I decide to go for him throughout the three remaining rounds. I mean – when will I even get another crack at a world title like this? But will my legs hold up? Yes, I am sure they will. I am thinking of all the roadwork I had been doing round Arthur's Seat in Edinburgh. It must count for something in these later stages of the fight. Even those hills in Merthyr Tydfil, surely they will count for something now. The fact of the matter is that every little extra step, extra round or extra hour out on the road came into play in those last three rounds. All the years of sacrifice were being called up to give a good account of themselves now. Three rounds between me and my dream. I go for it 'cause I know the fight is close.

It is now the fifteenth and final round. Laguna and me come out to the centre of the ring. We both look like a butcher has done a job on our faces with his meat cleaver. We touch gloves for the last time. I remember getting a sense of relief that it would soon be all over. I had gone through the limit of my physical endurance. Through the roof and out the other end. We catch each other's eyes for an instant as we touch gloves before getting on with the fight. There is respect in Laguna's eyes now. And to give him his due, it was his management that believed I was a patsy, not him. They put him in there believing he was to be fighting a patsy. We go at each other in that last round. Both of us throw everything we have – and more. The fight is very close and both of us believe we can win it. We are throwing as many punches as we can to catch the judges' eyes.

Half a minute to go and both of us are absolutely knackered, but we're not holding on. Both of us know that every punch counts. So we continue to throw punches with what we have left. We're in the middle of the ring – feet on the deck, rooted but still throwing punches. I keep saying to myself, *another jab Ken. And another. Keep going Ken. Let's go back to bonnie Scotland with the title. Come on.* The last thirty seconds of that fight seem to take longer than the rest of the fight put together. Ding ding ding ding ding, the bell goes to end the fight. Laguna and I hang on to each other having punched ourselves out. We can't even talk. I feel the dead weight of his body and he can feel mine. We're like two marathon dancers from the thirties. They shoot horses don't they?

The ring is invaded by officials and the police. The noise from the crowd is immense. I can't make out what they are saying or even begin to think about who they are screaming for. My dad is there and it is mayhem in that ring. I could really go a slug of the rep's magic orange drink now. There is a crackle and I can see the announcer clearing most of the ring so that he can make the announcement.

I am still trying to get my second breath back but my eyes are on the microphone. Somebody is listening to the Puerto Rican and translating it to me as it is said. I can't for the life of me remember who that was. The announcer says it's a split decision. I move over to my dad as the announcement is made. Laguna shuffles to his corner. The pause between the announcer saying split decision and the next word is gigantic. You could fit my whole life up to now in it. His mouth starts and the words start to come out again. Like slow motion in a movie. I am getting it all a split second behind the crowd through the translator. The judges have voted thus: two for me and one for Laguna. There's a pause while it sinks in.

Oh ya fuckin' beauty!

I jump up in the air – this time I am up there for a lifetime. I can see my dad's face far below smiling up at me. When I land I am champion of the world. 'I am champion! Dad – I am the world champion!'

Tears are flowing down my face. My dad and I are locked in arms together, crying. What I wanted all my life and what he wanted for me had come true. There we were – two ordinary men from ordinary backgrounds – in the middle of a Caribbean island – champions of the world. The both of us. The first words I remember uttering to him were, 'I hope Mum was watching, Dad.'

When he could stop his emotions for long enough to speak he said, 'Aye son I think you have made your mum very happy up there in heaven.'

It is a great day. My right eye is almost closed. My left eye has been closed since round eight. I can hardly see. But it is a great day. I don't feel any pain. My dad takes my arm to make sure I am walking the right direction away from the ring. Jack Solomons comes up and grabs me and gives me a big hug. 'Well done Ken you Scots git,' he says.

'No bad for a fuckin' patsy!' I say to him and he laughs.

We get back to the dressing-room for an interview with the press. The place is full of TV people and members of the press. My swelling eyes are in a terrible state. The swelling is going up and up, despite my dad applying an ice-pack to them between photos and questions. I am dreading the thought of my right eye closing. I'd be completely blind. But even if I was I'd be the happiest man alive and still the world champ.

Once the press conference was over I went into the bathroom and picked away some of the crusty blood around the cut. I got a bit off that opened the cut and the pressurised blood came squirting out. Freeing the blood stops the swelling, and I even felt the pressure easing off as the blood comes out. It eased the eye a bit but I was still having difficulty seeing. But all the blood and cuts in the world can't take this feeling away.

After the conference I was driven back to the La Concha Hotel where I was warmly greeted by the staff and customers. They all wanted my autograph or a photo taken with the new world champion. I was famous in a country I had never been to before. Yet I couldn't wait to get back to Scotland. Once I got to my hotel room I ordered a bucket full of ice. I applied it to my face to help bring down the swelling and the bruising around my cuts. I was hoping for a face that would be at least presentable for the victory dinner. That event would be at eight o'clock. I phoned Carol and told her the news – she was over the moon. Everything was looking rosy. Life had never been any better.

I looked at my face in the bathroom mirror. The bruising and swelling were at their worst. My left eye was completely closed and my right eye was just a little slit. The cut above my left eye was stitched up. Somebody knocked at the door – it was Jack. He told me to hurry up and get downstairs as everybody was waiting for me. I said I didn't feel up to it as my face was a mess.

Jack phoned downtairs and a few minutes later a waiter knocked on the door. Jack came in with a pot of women's make-up in his hand and smeared the cool cream on my face. A few minutes later he told me to look in the mirror. Good Lord! All the bruising had disappeared and I didn't look as if I had been in a fight at all.

Off we went to the banquet being held in the hotel. I received a warm welcome from the people who were dining in the restaurant that night, and many came up and shook my hand. As the night went on I started to feel my face going a bit hard, and I turned to my dad and asked him how I looked. My dad ran his hand over my cheeks, saying, 'That cream Jack's put on your face has gone brick hard.' I says, 'I know 'cause you'll have noticed that I can hardly talk correct.' By this time my right eye had closed as well and I was blind. I had to ask Dad to take me back to my room. Imagine, world champion and having to be led to my room by the hand!

My dad ran a shower for me and I stepped in and washed the make-up off my face. When I tried to put my head on the pillow it hurt 'cause Ismael had caught me some good head punches. My dad bent the pillows over so as my head dangled free of any contact. And that's how I slept all night.

a champion's welcome

When the plane touched down in Edinburgh I looked in a mirror at my face. I was still buzzing and it was still sinking in that I was champion. It didn't look too bad – good enough to face the press. I had rehearsed inside my head what I was going to say to them. How I had gone halfway round the world and brought the world title back to Scotland. Bonnie Scotland.

Coming down the steps from the plane, I was immediately met by my wife Carol and our twelve-day old son, Mark. It was one of the happiest moments of my life. My wife and son were going to want for nothing. Their lives were going to be rosy. I didn't get a king's ransom for the title fight, but there would be big purses in defending my title. As I held my new son, I scanned the place, half looking for the press. It took me a few seconds to realise that the airport was devoid of the press. Scotland had a world champion and only a few friends turned up to welcome me home. I wasn't on an ego trip. I mean, I had done something big, won a world title. I felt let down, thinking the country I loved so much had snubbed me.

I had a strange bag of emotions in that terminal. One Ken is the happiest man alive. The other Ken's unhappy, because he fought so hard for his new son, for Edinburgh and for Scotland. And only a couple of friends and my aunts and uncles were there to meet me. But I pushed it from my mind and went on to enjoy the rest of the day with my family and friends.

The next day I learned that nobody had known about the fight, none of the general public that is. The Scottish papers practically ignored it. There was a wee bit here and there in some of the papers. I might have still felt bitter at the media – choosing to ignore a world champion – but then that sort of thing happens across the board in Scottish media. It's a big village and I've always felt there is just too much envy floating about. I didn't feel so bad at the general public not turning up. How can people turn up to congratulate you if they know nothing about it? But people got to know. Slowly, the news got around.

Once it started ringing, the telephone never stopped. It was at this moment I should have got myself an agent to take the pressure off me. But I didn't. Maybe my life would have turned out different if I had had somebody to arrange dates, times and my fees. Here I was in the limelight, like a fish on a bike. I didn't know what to do. So I took all sorts of engagements on willy-nilly. I even paid for my own transport to events and back. I was hardly ever paid – in my naïveté I thought that was the way of things. The people who booked me should have known better.

Although I was world champion it didn't change my lifestyle too much. I was only paid £4,000. So when my manager took his cut from it, and I'd covered all my other expenses for the last two months, I wasn't exactly rolling in the money.

However, I took Carol on a holiday to Majorca. Mark was only a few weeks old so Carol's mum and dad, Anne and Frank, looked after him. They said Carol and I should get a nice wee break together. Funny thing about this wee break – Carol caught food poisoning. The doctor gave her an injection and told her to stay in bed for two days. A few days into the holiday a couple of English lads recognised me. Christ, no wonder! Both my eyes were bruised and stitched up. I posed for photographs with them and some with the waiters and hotel residents.

It took several weeks for me to finally get over the bumps and bruises from the fight. And a bit longer than that for the cut over my left eye finally to heal up. There's nothing like a bit of inactivity to let you know how much you need movement in your life. By the time a few weeks had passed I was itching to get back into the gym; I think my body had become addicted to physical endurance.

A phone call from Eddie Thomas brought a sparkle to my eyes. Jack Solomons had arranged something with Harry Markson, the president of Madison Square Garden. They wanted me to come over to New York and fight at another venue in the city. I was to box Donato Paduano the undefeated welterweight champion of Canada. And the great thing for me was I was to be on the same bill as Muhammad Ali. Ali – floats like a butterfly and stings like a bee – and me on the same bill. Great. Ali was to fight Oscar Bonavena. The date was to be sometime in December 1970.

You would think it might worry me that Paduano was a welterweight, and they made the fight at ten stone six pounds. Well, as I have been saying, I always hovered about the nine stone nine pounds area – and – as in Puerto Rico – with hot weather or extra training I find it hard to keep up at that weight. If I took the fight in Madison Square Garden I'd be giving away almost a stone in weight. But Paduano was a couple of inches shorter than me and not considered a big puncher. That helped me to make my mind up. But the main reason for my accepting that fight was that I'd be on the same bill as Ali: the greatest.

Jack Solomons asked if I wanted to watch some film of Paduano. I have never been one to watch films of the guy I am going to fight. What for? He should worry what I was going to do to him. I always wanted my opponent to change his style rather than me. Too many boxers think more about what the other guy can do. The TV and videos hype this up. The best advice I can give them is get in there and do what you do best in your own style.

At the weigh-in, Paduano came in at exactly ten stone six pounds. And by the build of him he must have had trouble making it. I was nine stone ten pounds. I had managed to go away up to the dizzy heights of one pound more than my normal fighting weight. That gave a ten-pound advantage to Paduano, but at this weight I wonder if it is right to call it an advantage. I was obviously going to be the faster boxer. And if it was right what they said – that Paduano was not a big hitter – then where was the advantage? I would say that the lighter boxer would have that, if the fight went over any distance. Another thing I knew – he had not been in the ring with anybody as fast as me. Nor had he been in with somebody who could use the full size of the ring. I aimed to get in there and move about – hitting him fast and accurate. Score points. Make him come to me all the time. Tire him out and then go in for the kill.

I was in my dressing-room and the door opens. In comes Angelo Dundee. 'Kenny – do you mind if Ali shares your dressing-room?'

I thought it was some kind of wind-up by my team. 'Get away!' I said, sure that he was taking the piss. But he wasn't. He said, 'No, no, Ali hasn't been allocated a room.'

That was the first time I had been in Madison Square Garden. And, from a boxer's point of view, once you have boxed there you can die in peace. When Ali came in he was brilliant. Full of that magic patter and quick wit he was famous for. And the funny thing was, I was top of the bill. I was world champion but I never felt that I was the world champion next to such a great man as Ali. Even though Ali wasn't the champ at that time. But we had a great laugh me and him. I drew an imaginary line in the middle of the room and said, 'Don't cross that line or there will be trouble.' Everybody in the room started laughing, and that broke the ice.

He crossed it and I had to push him back. 'I'm top of the bill tonight. When you are top of the bill you can come into my half of the dressing-room,' I joked.

Ali went away kidding on he was in the huff. Then the banter started up again. It was a great way to get my mind right for the fight. And the fight was the same at the first round as it was in the tenth. The pattern never changed. Paduano knew he had the weight advantage and kept coming forward. I kept picking him off and getting out of his way. Things were going exactly the way I had planned. He tried everything in the book to get me to stand still and fight toe to toe. No way I was going to do that. You lose the head, you lose the fight. I kept doing what I was doing best and continued scoring the points. I could see that my style was starting to frustrate him. Now and then he came in with some wild punches, but they never connected. I simply stepped back, then I'd lean in with a jab or a quick combination if I thought I could get away with it. As we went into the last couple of rounds, I was well ahead on points. I knew I had it in the bag. I just jabbed and moved till the bell rang at the end of every round. I was fit but my fitness was never fully tested. It was one of the most technical fights I have ever been in. I won on all the judges' scorecards.

Just how fit I was can be shown by the fact I'd caught a cold the day before the fight. I'd gone to the gym for a session of skipping and sparring, but because of a taxi strike, we had hung around outside the gym for ages in the freezing cold, still sweating from the work, before finally deciding to walk back to the hotel. My dad and I shared a room, and during the night he heard me tossing and turning so he got up to see how I was. My pyjamas were soaking with sweat. I took them off and he rubbed me down, before I put on a new pair. In the last round of the fight, the cold finally began to have its effect – it was the only one I lost in the contest.

I received wonderful applause from the packed audience. They seemed to appreciate my boxing style. I was going to enjoy boxing in America. I hoped my success would attract more top Brits over there to fight. But they seemed to be content boxing in London till my good pal John H. Stracey went to Mexico and beat José Napoles for the world welterweight title.

I remember well the times I sparred with John in Terry Lawless's gym in London. There is nothing like a few hundred rounds of sparring to build up a solid friendship. It was always great training and experience for me. We were both good left jabbers but John was that bit of a bigger hitter than me. You didn't want to be caught on the chin with one of them. No, sir. I had to slip his jab as much as I could, especially since John was a stone heavier than me, and he was then knocking on the British champion's door. We had that in common: a focus, a place where we wanted to be, a dream. Maybe that's what bonded us more than all the sparring?

I had picked up some good pointers sparring in the gyms over in the States. I sparred mostly with guys who were bigger and heavier than me. John was just that little bit different. He had an edge – it's hard to explain but there was something there that was missing in most of the other sparring partners I had. John was young, keen and eager to get on. The night John stopped José Napoles for the world welterweight title was fabulous. Here was a boxer who committed himself to becoming the best in the world. And that's what he became. He knew what it meant to give up going out with the boys or girls, leaving the drink alone. Not that John drank much – but the sacrifice was there. He toed the line. This is what a boxer must do if he really wants to be a good champion. He must toe the line in every area of life. Nothing must be left to chance.

I was soon home again pottering about, working out at the gym when I received a telephone call from Ray Clarke of the British Boxing Board of Control in London. He wanted to know if I'd go over to Los Angeles and fight Mando Ramos for the vacant WBC title. If I won it, the British Boxing Board of Control would recognise me as undisputed champion of the world. Fuckin' brilliant! Nip over to America Ken, knock the shit out of this American opponent, come home safe and sound: undisputed champion. Now the BBBC would surely take some sort of notice of that.

For when I went to San Juan, I'd won only the WBA version of the title by beating Laguna, but the British Boxing Board of Control, who were affiliated to the WBC, refused to recognise me, although the WBA recognised me as the new world lightweight champion. I must admit I was a bit bitter about all this and Eddie Thomas issued a writ against the British Boxing Board of Control. Still, there was a way to stop the arguments: beat whatever rival world contender they chose to put in with me. I was learning that there was more to boxing than just throwing punches. Laguna had found the same thing, too, for he was stripped of his WBC title just ahead of our fight. So he ended up losing one version to me and the other to the administrators.

I was to box Mando Ramos who was the ex-champion, but about seven days before the fight, Ramos called it off. His manager said it was due to a groin strain, and the locals clearly knew he was not going to be fit for the fight as they had already started calling their bets off. The promoter, Aileen Eaton, pro-duced Ruben Navarro, then rated number five in the world. He had been in training for an eliminator for the title, so it was clear that I wasn't being handed a patsy. (In fact Aileen Eaton had known that Ramos might not be fit so she had been on the lookout for a top contender to fill his boots.)

I started off my training at the Sparta with my dad. Nobody could take the edge off it if I was undisputed champion of the world. At first, I worked out with the amateurs following their training session – I also sparred with some of them which is what I normally did. That got me up to a reasonable level of fitness. But the last three weeks before I flew out to Los Angeles I had a couple of welterweights flown up from London. It was time to step up a gear. My schedule was getting tighter and tighter. I was honing my life down so that all there was, was me and that fight at the end of my training.

My schedule started at seven in the morning, running round Arthur's Seat. The hills seemed to be the best thing for me. They took a lot out of you. Any boxer knows that once you're fit you can run on the flat all day long. But put a couple of hills in there and that will separate the men from the boys. The sweat would be running out of me and I'd jog back home and into a bath. I'd relax and then go back to bed till one o'clock. I'd get up and have a light high-protein lunch, chicken or steak – that sort of stuff. I was getting really fit.

I'd rest most of the day watching movies, or playing the odd game of golf. It might seem like a pretty regimented way of life, but if I was ever getting fed up with it I'd just imagine what it must be like working day in and day out in a factory or a steelworks or shipyard. That sure made me appreciate the privileged position I had found myself in. After lounging about all day living the life of Riley, in the evening I'd go to the gym and have a strenuous work-out. I worked harder and harder as the time drew nearer the fight. Suddenly there it was: I was on my way to Los Angeles with my dad and Eddie. It seemed we were never off planes in those days. Every time I got on a plane I remembered Dick McTaggart asking Bobby Mallin to wind the window down – and I'd laugh and my dad or Eddie would ask what I was laughing at. *Aw! Nothing!* I'd say because I had told them the story a million times.

On arriving in Los Angeles we were met by a group of Scottish immigrants. They had formed the Scots American Club. It was a great sight to see them all decked out in kilts and sporrans and with bagpipes. They lined up at the bottom of the steps and piped us off the plane in all the regalia. It was a wonderful reception.

We booked into our hotel, though I can't remember much about it because I had been in so many, when I try to remember them they all merge into the one. For the next two weeks I ran in the mornings and went to the gym in the early evening. The running reminded me of the Puerto Rico early morning runs. There were crickets and palm trees and that same tropical smell.

Los Angeles was a pleasant place and everybody seemed cheerful enough waving and saying hi. Jogging had caught on in a big way in the States by then, but it was still unusual to see anybody out jogging in Scotland. Although there isn't much I can remember about the hotel there is one thing I do remember: an earthquake.

It was a few days before the fight, and I was winding down on my training. I had been fast asleep when I was woken up by the bed moving. I was a bit confused as to what was going on, but as I came out from underneath the covers, I noticed my bed was shaking, and so was the table in my room. Christ, I thought, what's going on here? Outside I heard smashing glass and some screams, so I got out of bed and looked out the window: the hotel swimming pool's water looked like tidal waves as it swished from one side to the other. Then, just as suddenly, it all stopped.

As I was up, I thought I may as well go out on my run, even though it was still early. While running down the street I had to stay in the middle of the road, because there was debris every-where: broken glass, dustbins, branches that had fallen from trees – the lot. I ran for about forty-five minutes, and as I was returning to the hotel I noticed my dad and Eddie standing by the entrance.

'Kenny, where the hell have you been?' my dad asked. I started to laugh. Here I was in my running gear, sweat dripping off my face, and he asks me where I've been! Dad told me that when he woke up and heard people running and shouting along the corridor, he realised something was up so he went to my room to check I was all right. As I wasn't there, he and Eddie were worried that I might get hit by a falling stone or some glass. It was going to take more than an earthquake to distract us.

In the Los Angeles gym I had my pick of the sparring partners. Boxing in this part of Los Angeles is very big, because it is a poor area, and they always have a big boxing fraternity. I had plenty of good opposition to choose from. They were queuing up to spar with me. I was after all the world champion. This one day I was sparring away, trying to get as best a workout from the session as I could. There was nothing different about this session until my partner threw a wild punch. I put that down to a slip of the mind. But then he did it again. I let it go, thinking he was just showing off to his mates. But when he tried it again I started to get suspicious. You see even though you go pretty hard at it in sparring there is an unwritten law that you don't try to knock each other's heads off. You're in there to help each other, especially the one who is training for a big fight. The last thing you want to do is injure him so that he'd have to cancel the fight and so lose his purse and maybe his reputation. Trying to injure a man during sparring is like stealing a joiner's toolbag – the outcome of which is that he can no longer make any money.

Well this day, with this particular sparring partner, I noticed he was doing everything he could to knock me out. He was trying to show me up – coming in with fancy combinations when it was obvious who was in charge in the ring. Normally you would allow your sparring partner to finish his combination before laying into him. This guy was going for me in a big way. I think he was trying to cut me because his head came in too close for comfort a couple of times too. But I guess I was too fast on my feet. No way was he making an arse of me – I turned up the volume on him and you could see that he was shocked.

We found out later on that he was sent in to find out how good I was. Posing as a sparring partner, he was a spy from Navarro's manager who also managed him. He didn't get to do much spying after I decked him in the second round. That didn't give him much to talk about when he went back to his boss. After that I was a bit wary as to who I sparred with. But there were no problems from anybody, just a wee nod from our camp over to Navarro's camp to let them know that we knew what they had been up to with the sparring spy. So everything was hunky dory. The stage was set and I was ready to win both the WBC and the WBA titles and take them back to Scotland as undisputed champion.

At ringside somebody tried the dope-bottle trick on us. Luckily my dad spotted it. It was a plastic bottle that had been flung into the ring, just at that spot where a second might reach out and pick it up as the fighter was coming back to the stool during the minute rest period between rounds. My dad opened it and sniffed it. He recoiled. 'A bad liquid,' was all he said. It had been our intention to hand it over to the authorities for testing as soon as the fight was over, but somebody spirited it away. You always half expected an attempt would be made to dope you, as there are always people who want to fix a fight. That's why all our bottles were carefully guarded. The bottles and corks were covered in marked tape. Even more to the point – our bottles were glass so there was less chance of a plastic one slipping through our guard. It's hard to tell who might try that trick with the bottle. It might be the manager of the opponent. It might be the boss of a betting syndicate. But it might just as well be an ordinary punter who has stuck a right few quid on Navarro. There is no way of telling.

Navarro came out in the first round throwing leather. He wanted to impress me from the start. He caught me with a good punch on my left ear. I later learned from a specialist that the punch had perforated my eardrum, and that I might need an operation. Strangely my only concern about this was a holiday in the Canaries that we had planned: I wouldn't now be able to go swimming.

Anyway – back to the fight. Navarro proved to be one of the roughest fighters I had met up until then. The referee was good and warned Navarro several times but he still got in some kidney punches and caught me low. Navarro would crouch low then come up throwing all different kinds of hooks and upper cuts. Like a jack-in-the-box – that's what he was like. So it was going to be a different sort of fight from my usual. I don't know why he chose to fight in that style because most of his punches were thrown while he was off balance because he was crouching and coming up with them and I was moving about the ring. I think it was because I was never where his brain thought I'd be when he started throwing the punch. I decided to keep moving about the ring in case he caught me with a lucky swing.

Had I not paced myself so carefully I think I could have stopped Navarro before the end of the fight. I didn't give him time to settle down. He always seemed like a man who was trying to work his way into the fight. And as I have told you before – I never change my tactics to suit the man I am boxing. So Navarro spent the whole of the fight trying to find a way to pin me down. A way to get me to stand and fight him. You can imagine how that fight went. The first round was very much like the last one. Every round consisted of Navarro coming forward trying to land the big one and me picking him off. I wasn't concerned about knocking him out. I just kept on scoring points. Jab jab – combinations. Points all the time. I wanted to win as easily as possible and not get involved in a brawl. The longer the fight went on, the more Navarro tried to mug me. The more he tried to mug me, the more I stepped away scoring points. By halfway through the fight I knew that – barring a mishap – I would win the title.

When the bell rang for the end of the last round there was only one winner on the cards. Me. I had become the undisputed champion of the world. And if some people in the boxing world had thought I was a patsy before the Laguna fight, and maybe lucky after the Laguna fight – they had to realise now that I was a fighter to be reckoned with.

I'd come from a hard British title defence to this in a very short time. To me it was like a rocket to the moon. Surely the media in Scotland would have to take notice now. They would have to wake up to what I had achieved. I'd come all this way from a pre-fab in Edinburgh. A wee eight-year-old with a pair of boxing-gloves I had got from my aunt Agnes as a Christmas present. From a back-garden boxer, I had become the first British fighter since Ted 'Kid' Lewis to win a world title in America. Lewis had succeeded fifty years before me. I was also the first

British fighter since Lewis to win a world title anywhere outside of Britain. And also the first British world lightweight champion since Freddie Welsh who had won the title in 1914 in London. Yet not much more than a year earlier I was out of boxing, disillusioned with the whole game. Only my mother's death had changed that, and I was sad that she did not live long enough to see me crowned world champion, so that was a moment for me that held mixed emotions. How I'd have loved my mum to have been at Edinburgh airport when I came home after the Navarro fight. I'd have given everything to see her smiling as I stepped off that plane with the world trophy in my hands. But alas that wasn't to be.

On the way back on the plane I hoped that at least some of the papers would have their photographers out there on the tarmac or in the terminal when we got to Edinburgh. I wasn't being big-headed – I just think I was due the publicity and acclaim that I deserved. I'd gone back to America and won the undisputed lightweight title. Surely they would afford me some coverage this time?

I knew there was something different when my plane landed. The pilot announced: 'Would all passengers quickly leave their seats and go to the air terminal as there are some important people on board who have to leave the plane last.'

I looked out of the window – and boy did my heart take a leap. It was a better feeling than when I took the title from Navarro. The airport was packed. Hundreds of people all decked out in tartan. Some had my name on big posters and they were waving Scottish flags about. It brought a tear to my eye. In the crowd – if I looked carefully – I could see some of my relatives and pals and fans whose faces I recognised. I couldn't wait to get off and greet them all. What happened in this same airport after the Laguna fight was washed from my mind. This moment belonged to me and my fans.

I looked and the plane was nearly empty, but I noticed a several people holding back. From the way they were acting and the things they were saying you could tell that they thought it was them who were to stay back, that they were the important people who had to leave last. And why was that? Turns out they were Radio One DJs. One of them was Ed Stewart, though I didn't know that at the time.

In fact, Ed Stewart told me the story many years later. After the pilot's announcement, he and the other DJs looked out the window, saw all the fans and assumed the crowd had gathered for them. They hung about and they were actually wondering why I wasn't leaving the plane. Ed looked out the window, turned round to his fellow DJ and said, 'This is my first visit to Edinburgh and look at the reception!'

Of course it was a bit of a let-down when the pilot came up and asked them to leave the plane because there was a VIP who had to leave last. I told him about the previous time I had landed and nobody had turned up. Airports had given us both some embarrassing moments in the past.

I took a big breath and stepped out of the plane. There was a moment's silence and then a loud cheer. It was magic. It was just magic to share my success with all these people. It meant much more than just winning the world title. It gave it a meaning beyond me. I came off the plane and down the stairs and was met by the Lord Provost of Edinburgh, Kenneth Borthwick, a Portobello man like myself. 'Well done Ken,' he said. 'We're all very proud of you.'

I have had that said to me a million times in my life. But when somebody says it and they mean it, you know. The Provost meant he was proud of me, and the crowd was too. I don't think my achievement would have mattered as much as it did if it wasn't for that crowd. I'd like to take this opportunity to thank every single person who turned up at the airport that day, and along the route into Edinburgh. You have no idea how much it meant to me.

Och – there were tears in my eyes. I had stopped trying to hide them ages ago. I was like a big lassie. My family: aunts, uncles, cousins and lots of friends were there. My whole life was flashing before my eyes – only I was more alive than I had ever been. I was going through the crowd shaking hand after hand. People were slapping me on the back. *Well done Ken – you showed them Ken – you're some man Ken.*

It fair took my breath away. I felt like a pop star. When the Bay City Rollers came back through this same airport a few years later and I saw them on the telly, I was laughing because I knew what they felt like.

I met my good friend Ted Hendy, the duty officer at the airport. Ted made sure I got through the crowd and into the terminal. Eventually. I didn't mind shaking hands and signing autographs. But Ted was intent on getting me off the tarmac and into the terminal before I got run down by a plane.

It was some sight. I'd never seen anything like it. The building was jam-packed with people, and there were tartan scarves everywhere. People had caught on to my tartan shorts. A lot of Irish boxers used to fight with a shamrock on their shorts, but you never seen a Scottish boxer wearing tartan shorts until then. I wore them because I loved Scotland. I waded through the sea of people. The whole thing was exactly what I would have wanted it to be – but more. The singing and the bagpipes playing – it was great.

It was an ocean of tartan. I'd only seen that much tartan at Scotland football games. I pushed through the crowd and the cheers and chants and pats on the back. I whistled on a taxi but Ted laughed. 'There's your taxi there, Ken,' he said and nodded the other way.

I turned round and there was an open-topped bus. And you don't get many of them in Scotland. No sir – not with our weather. I was led on to the bus and behind me the chants of the crowd in the airport got louder and louder. For a minute I thought the roof was going to come off. If you want an idea of how loud it was – a big jet took off during the mayhem, yet you couldn't hear it over the noise of the crowd. It was like a fairy-tale. My whole boxing life rolled in front of me – from the wee boy at the Sparta to leaving the airport on an open-topped bus.

I remembered seeing this bus as a wee boy, going through the city with a football team in it, Heart of Midlothian or Hibernian, and some trophy or other. But it must have been lying idle for a while that bus – because Hearts or Hibs hardly ever won the Scottish Cup. My wife and family sat on the top deck with me and we were like the Royal Family. The Provost told me we were off to the City Chambers. There was a bit of a do waiting for me there. 'Christ – all this and a free meal too,' I said. 'Can't be bad.'

I decided to settle down if we were going to go all the way to the city centre. I had had my homecoming and I was delighted. I settled down – quite happy, no – over the moon in fact. I was over the moon – the reception was far beyond anything I had imagined.

But I didn't settle down for long. It soon became clear that the reception had only just begun. As we turned out on to the main road I thought I was seeing things. But as we got closer I realised that I wasn't. There were all these people lined along the streets. And sometimes I am daft. I was beginning to wonder what all these people were doing lined along the streets when it dawned on me – they were there to see me. All these people, strangers, there to wish me well. I remember the Provost smiling as he saw the realisation on my face. I felt like my ship had finally come in.

'You'd better stand up Ken son – they'll be expecting a wave at least.'

I stood up. I remember pressing against the barrier with my legs to keep steady. At that point you could have knocked me out with a left jab. We came down on to the Maybury roundabout, and a huge crowd was gathered there. In among them I could pick out my good pals Bill and Margaret Forsyth – they ran the Maybury Roadhouse. I tried shouting at them but they just kept waving and cheering like the rest of the people. They couldn't hear me. All their staff and customers were out too. I waved back. There was no point in trying to shout out to individual people, this was a crowd thing. A Scottish thing. I might have been the centre of it – but the day belonged to everybody. I turned to my dad and said, 'I wish Mum could have been here to see this.'

He just smiled and said, 'She is son. She is.'

And I suppose she was – I imagined her standing somewhere in that crowd. An anonymous woman cheering. On we went through the streets. And all along the route there were people. Scarves and banners hanging from windows. Cars going past with the horns tooting and people waving. I could see the headlines on the papers in shop doorways. 'Just Champion' – stuff like that. There was a great feeling in the air. Through Corstorphine we went – there were even people out there and you wouldn't think they would be big boxing fans. I mentioned that to the Provost and he said, 'Aye – maybe not Ken – but you can bet your bottom dollar they're big Scotland fans.' And there was no getting past that. This really was a big Scotland day.

Eventually we arrived at the start of Princes Street. If I thought I had seen it all already – but this was beyond belief. It took the wind right out of my sails. The street was packed with well-wishers. The bus had to nudge its way through them all. Slapping the side of the bus and shouting up to me. It would have brought a tear to a glass eye. It took us ages to travel that last half a mile. I definitely knew I had seen it all now, but when we got to the end of Princes Street and turned up towards the bridges the place was jam-packed with even more people. I couldn't believe the amount of people who had come out of a warm house to see me: Ken Buchanan.

We turned up into the High Street and into the City Chambers where the bus came to a halt. The City Chambers was alive with people. It looked like the building was hovering on the heads of all those people. I swear I have never seen so many people in the centre of Edinburgh since that. OK, the Bay City Rollers probably had a crowd like that, but I was too old to go along to see them. Although some of their songs were not bad at all. Shang a lang!

Anyway, this was my night, it was like Hogmanay. My own personal New Year's Eve. Every face I passed was blessed with a big smile. It was wonderful to see so many people happy. I remember wondering what would have happened if I had taken the route of my other talent: the bible prize. Imagine if I had been a minister. You would have to be God himself to gather a crowd like this on the streets of Edinburgh. And even then I am not too sure they would get out of their warm beds!

The rest of the night was a blur. I know we had a great meal, and speeches, and dancing and drinking. And more dancing. And more drinking. We partied right into the next day. One flashback is me on the way home and a couple of guys staggering along the street chanting Ken Buchaaaaa – nan! Ken Buchaaaaa – nan! They went right past me chanting without recognising me. That was funny. The next thing I remember is my wife taking my shoes off and lifting my legs into the bed. I was certain to have a big hangover when I woke up. And boy did I.

management problems

After a couple of days Eddie Thomas called me. He wanted to settle the purse I had won at the fight. I was all for that. In the excitement I had nearly forgot about the money. The total purse was $60,000. Not bad for a night's work I was thinking, but Eddie said he was taking $20,000 as his cut.

I argued that according to our contract he was entitled to only twenty-five per cent after expenses and ten per cent to my trainer were taken off. That was the usual settlement for all boxers and managers in Britain. Eddie told me he had worked hard on this fight and he had earned the extra money. I wondered if this meant he hadn't worked as hard on other fights when he took the normal twenty-five per cent?

I should explain here how a boxer's purse is arranged, as money issues frequently crop up in the sport. There are differences between American and British contracts. At the time in America, the contract between a boxer and a manager stated that the manager was allowed to take thirty-three per cent of the boxer's purse if he wanted to. If he *wants* to. In a British contract, the manager was allowed to take only twenty-five per cent. When I first agreed to an American contract with Eddie for my only title fight in the States in September 1970 I signed it only when Eddie agreed to take the twenty-five per cent commission as stipulated in the British contract – after expenses are taken off.

I was hurt, to say the least, that he had decided to change

things without consulting me. How could this man I had trusted for so long suddenly start asking for more than we had agreed. Looking back now I can see I had a lot to learn. As I said, there was more to boxing than just throwing punches. It was me who had done all the hard work. Training myself into the ground – with the help of my dad of course. Where was Eddie on all the long miles and round after round in the gym? Eddie wasn't my trainer, but many people came to think that he was. My dad had always been my trainer. Eddie had little to do with my training routine, though he was happy to let people believe that he had. His role there finished at the beginning of 1969, right after my fight with Ameur Lamine in Hamilton, at the end of the previous year.

I decided if Eddie and I were going to work together it would be on the terms I had signed in the first place. I told him he was entitled to only twenty-five per cent, as agreed, but Eddie said he was only carrying out what it said on the contract. I argued back that we had a deal based on twenty-five per cent. He kept talking about the contract, though we clearly had very different ideas about what it meant. Because of this, I lost my trust in him, as I felt he was trying to take advantage of me.

It was effectively the beginning of the end of our relationship, though I had eight months left of my contract with Eddie and I wanted to fulfil that as promised. My motto has always been: never make a promise and not keep it.

Still, other opportunities quickly came my way, as other managers saw the potential of having a world champion on their books. Jarvis Astaire, a prominent boxing manager in London, phoned me, wanting to know if I'd be interested in boxing at Wembley indoors in May? 'Sure,' I said. 'So long as the purse is right.'

But it turned out that there were difficulties in doing a deal between the London promoters and Eddie as they had had difficulties going back over several years.

Jarvis had a solution. He said, 'Let's you and myself agree on an opponent and purse. I'll ring Harry Levene and tell him to phone Eddie and give him the match and the money – then everything will be OK.'

Appearing at Wembley on a big bill as the world champion in a non-title bout would be good for me. I could have a good pay day and show the British supporters a world champion in action. After a bit of chat, Jarvis and I agreed that I would fight Carlos Hernandez. Hernandez was the former world light-welterweight champion. He was a good strong opponent, and I'd be paid £8,000. That seemed a good enough purse for me so I let Jarvis get on with the arrangements – he'd get right on the blower to Harry Levene who, in turn, would call Eddie. The next day I received a call from Eddie saying Harry Levene had been on the phone asking if I'd be interested in boxing Carlos Hernandez at Wembley Arena for £6,000! Somewhere along the line, my purse had been reduced, but I never let on that I knew I could get £2,000 more, and that I thought Eddie was pulling a fast one. I said to Eddie, 'No – I am not fighting for six grand, but if the offer is for eight thousand then he has himself a deal.'

There was a pause then Eddie said he'd see what he could do. Perhaps he was just trying to show me what a good negotiator he was, after our recent fallout. We left it at that. I couldn't help but laugh when I got off the phone. Somebody somewhere was as fly as a jailer. I phoned Jarvis to tell him what had happened, and he assured me that within the hour Eddie would be back on the phone to me, and this time the money would be sorted. Sure enough half an hour later Eddie rang saying Harry was now offering £8,000. There was a pause and you could tell that Eddie wanted me to thank him for getting that extra two grand for me, but I said nothing as I had the purse I wanted. I was going to be fighting in the Wembley Arena. If it wasn't for Jarvis Astaire setting this up then Britain would never have seen me fight as world champion. Thanks Jarvis.

I trained as always for the fight for I knew that boxing Carlos Hernandez would be a fair challenge. It turned out he was perfect for me. He was bigger – I've always liked that. His left hand was always kept low. I don't know how he got away with that in other fights. How he got to this level fighting like that, leaving himself so open. But then Ali boxed like that too, and see how successful he was. That one flaw allowed me to pick him off with snappy jabs and even right-handers in over the top of his jab. The fight was going my way early on. Then I caught him with some good combinations in the seventh round. I could see that I had shaken him. When the bell rang he went back to his corner unsteady on his feet, I knew he had been hurt but in a clash of heads I got a cut above my left eye, which meant I had to postpone my rematch against Laguna. When he came out for the eighth round I moved in and threw a quick burst of punches. He went back and was unable to defend himself. He didn't go down so I kept going. I was glad when the referee jumped in to stop him from further punishment. Sometimes the referees were a bit slow at intervening. You knew your opponent had nothing left and he knew, but the referee didn't. And you can't stop punching. But here Hernandez was saved from further punishment.

I had invited two of the lads from the Trefoil School for handicapped and blind children in Ratho to fly down to the fight with a nurse each. I remember catching glimpses of them now and then as the rounds ended or began. After the fight we had a good chat. They were amazed: the flight down, the lights and cameras, the fight, the crowd – it was an experience they would never forget, they said. I was just happy to do something for people less fortunate than myself.

As usual after the fight we all went out for a slap-up meal. I had just seen that fight as a pay day and a chance for the rest of Britain to see their world champion. I wanted to be back home and spend some time with my family. Then the good bit – home to my ain folk. That is where you come down to reality. Get your

feet firmly on the ground again. It's good to be among your own –
because the buzz up in that ring can be very heavy. The come-
down can be rapid but they are always there to catch you.

Once I was back to normality, out on the golf course with a
couple of my pals or my dad, I could relax and go with the flow of
things. I knew I was no golfer but just being out there was good
for me. It brought me back down to earth, as I was no longer
being seen as world champion, but merely as Ken playing in the
monthly medal, or playing a round with another member of the
club. OK, that golfer may have been bursting to get back into the
clubhouse to announce he knocked me out of the competition,
boasting how he beat the world champion. But for me it was just a
laugh. I wonder how many people round the world have beat
world champions at sports the champions were rubbish at? I was
just happy to learn something from my opponents during our
games. If I could pick up a tip to make my golf that bit better than
I counted that as a successful game. Just the same as when I was
in America going round all the gyms watching and learning. Or in
Moscow all those years ago when I didn't do too well myself but
picked up hundreds of tips from the experienced boxers who were
there. Watching and learning. I might have improved my boxing
with this technique, but my golf still leaves a lot to be desired.

About this time the papers began to ask where and when my
next bout would be. They were making all sorts of crazy compari-
sons between me and other living boxers, or dead boxers – even
imaginary boxers. They were also hoping I would defend my
world title in Edinburgh. And to tell the truth, so did I. I loved the
idea of defending my title in front of a home crowd. Dad thought
it was a great idea too. Especially to repay the crowds that came
to welcome me at the airport. Ordinary folk who went out their
road to make sure I had a great homecoming. But I was never to
fight in Edinburgh as a professional.

My dad had an idea: where is the biggest and best stadium in
Edinburgh? The next day off we went up to Murrayfield ice rink.

But it also doubled up as the biggest indoor stadium in Edinburgh – at that time anyway. We had already phoned the manager about our idea and he was there waiting in his office. I told him that I had just become the undisputed lightweight champion of the world and asked him what were the chances of holding a world title bout on his premises. I couldn't believe it when he refused. I mean – we thought we were doing him a favour. It's not every day you get the chance of a world title fight in your premises is it?

He says he couldn't rent the stadium out as it would mean cancelling the ice skating or curling that night. At first I thought he was joking. I grinned – good one! I was about to say. I was waiting for him to get serious when he got up from his table and walked us to the door. He was sorry that he couldn't be more helpful. Couldn't be more helpful? He couldn't have been less helpful. My dad could see that I was mad – that I wanted to say something but he gave me the nod to keep it quiet and we said thanks and left. Boy was I mad. I go out of my way to do the guy a favour and he shuns me. I couldn't believe he wouldn't cancel the curling in my home town to allow me to defend my world title there. Sometimes Scotland has found it hard to accept its heroes. But my dad pointed out it's probably not just in Scotland, but in Outer Mongolia, or Nebraska. Somebody in Atlanta could handle a boxer from Nebraska winning the world title – but they might not be too keen on one from Atlanta. It's just that many places struggle to accept a person from their own area becoming celebrities of any sort. Scotland isn't a big enough place to accept heroes. There's always somebody that knows somebody that knows you, and small places can breed envy. So that was that – goodbye Scotland – America here I come again!

And I was to be off to America sooner than I thought. Eddie phoned all cheery to tell me that Teddy Brenner from Madison Square Garden was on the phone to Jack Solomons asking if Ken Buchanan would be at all interested in defending his title against his old opponent Ismael Laguna in September in The Gardens.

'So long as they don't have to cancel the skating,' I said.

'What?' Eddie said.

'Nothing. When do we leave?'

Well, I had fought Laguna in the searing Puerto Rican heat – surely I could beat him in the relative cool of Madison Square Garden? It was one fight I wanted to take: I believed I could beat him again, there was money to be made – my purse was $100,000 as champion, around ten times as much as I'd got as a challenger.

The fight was soon all fixed up. And I was going to be top of the bill at Madison Square Garden. I felt that although I couldn't even get a fight in my home town I was still top of the bill in the greatest city in the world. So it was great news for me. I couldn't believe it. Top of the bill is one thing – but top of the bill in Madison Square Garden – well – that is another thing altogether. It was also something a Scotsman had never done before. I was to boldly go where no Scotsman has gone before. Beam me up Scotty.

I had last boxed in New York in December 1970, on the same bill as Muhammad Ali. He fought Oscar Bonavena from Argentina and I fought Donato Paduano from Canada. I thought I had gone down well with the boxing people in New York. The crowd had liked me and given me a standing ovation. They had appreciated a technical boxer, but this was going to be a much harder contest than the Paduano fight. Laguna was coming to win back the title from me. He would be in a much sharper mental state this time – now that he knew I was not a patsy. And one thing was for sure – I'd be well paid by the New York boys. Certainly no British promoter had made me an offer. No point in hanging about in Britain waiting for a big purse to come my way.

I started training as usual at the Sparta. A new generation of boys had started moving through the amateur world. I was only too happy to give them tips and a wee spar whenever they asked. I was soon back into the old routine again. A strict regime. It was roadwork in the mornings and the gym at night. In the gym I'd start off with three rounds of shadow-boxing. It's amazing – there comes a time in a work-out when your whole body feels warm and lubricated. There is no friction at all in the joints. Your breathing levels out and you feel great, like you could go on forever. I liked that feeling.

After the shadow-boxing I went eight rounds with two good welterweights I brought up from London. I'd finish in the ring with two good rounds of fast punching on the hook and jab pads. Out the ring then for thirty minutes' skipping. Then I'd finish by doing my floor exercises – they included some light weights and the heavy medicine ball. I don't know why they call it a medicine ball, perhaps because when you get hit by it you need some medicine to recover.

As the hype before the fight built up I moved my training to Maybury Roadhouse. Bill and Margaret Forsyth made me more than welcome. It was good for their trade to have me training there. And I liked it. So they were doing me a favour and I was doing them one. They sold tickets to come in and watch me training, and the money from the ticket sales went to help the Blind School at Ratho. Once you're into a training session like this you hardly notice the people watching. I didn't mind people watching me so long as it benefited people who were unable to do so.

Two weeks before the fight I flew off to the States. I was to finish my training at Grossingers in the Catskill Mountains, a range about eighty miles from New York. What a place – talk about posh. It made Barnton look like an inner-city slum. This was your millionaires' paradise, where the rich and famous came to relax and enjoy themselves. Rocky Marciano used to train there way back in the sixties so at least it had some sort of boxing pedigree. There is something about the rich and their flirtation with boxing I have never been able to understand. I mean there are always plenty of rich folk hanging about the pre-fight gyms and at the ringside and press conferences and after-fight dinners.

But I am always asking myself this question: How many kids from rich backgrounds do you ever meet at the boxing gyms? Answer: almost none! The gym up in the Catskill Mountains was no different. They were there all right. Smoking cigars and discussing boxing like they had been professional boxers for ten years. I absorbed myself in my training. And this was a great place to do it. It had all the equipment you needed and more. Against one of the walls there was this heavy bag. Nobody would hit the thing because it was so hard. It was like the trunk of a tree and they called it Rocky after their famous guest.

I was well into a good routine and five days a week I'd get up at six in the morning and run for an hour. It was some place. Stunning to look at. And by now I had been to a few places round the world – but this landscape took some beating. I'd run right out around the golf course, which was very hilly. Every day I turned up the pressure on myself. Went that wee bit longer – faster – harder. I'd be bombing along there and wishing I could just be a guy strolling through the greens. Whacking the ball and following it at a right leisurely pace, maybe putting for a couple of birdies. Instead of pounding out the miles on the road, I could be just Ken. Ken playing a game of golf with his American buddies. But that's not the way to be thinking before a fight. Not before any fight, never mind a world title fight. And especially not before a world title fight where your opponent has come to take back the title you took from him. When I caught my head doing that kind of thinking, I'd shake it off and get my mind focused on the job at hand. Ismael Laguna – my old pal. It was easy to sleep breathing in that clean mountain air. There's something about mountain air that makes you sleep deep and sound. After roadwork and a quick sleep, I'd usually wake up about half eleven. Down the stairs for a light breakfast – scrambled eggs with toast and honey. I'd always take my cod liver oil and salt tablets before eating, so I knew they would be in my stomach first, putting back some of the goodness I'd lost sweating on my run. I always felt that the cod liver oil helped lubricate my joints and muscles, helping me move more fluidly in the ring. While the salt tablets would deal with the sweating.

It's hard to imagine what a top fighter goes through. What enables him to push to the limit during a fight. The training for top-level boxing is probably the hardest training in any sport. I always made sure the ringside commentator couldn't say I was tiring, or that I was letting the fight slip away because I wasn't fit. I made sure I was always in the best of condition. And I did that by going that extra bit in training, running that other mile, going that wee bit faster, throwing those extra punches in sparring.

Whatever it took, I kept on raising the stakes for myself, especially with what many people believed to be my unorthodox training methods, such as my underwater swimming.

Whether I was in training or not I went to the baths at least twice a week. I have already spoken about that a bit, but it's that good it deserves some more. In fact I might start doing it again now, to help steer me into old age with a bit of finesse. I would dive in at one end of the pool and swim up and back without surfacing: two lengths underwater. I'm quite proud of that in a funny kind of way. Not too many people could do that. But I was to top that. Like moving from the British title to the world title in boxing. My underwater glory was to come in the new Commonwealth pool when it opened in Edinburgh. I decided it was a challenge to my underwater abilities. Off I went for a look – Pheww! It was one big pool. I had to go for it. Me versus that rectangle of blue water. Sometimes I just think I am plain crazy, but you have got to be a bit crazy to get through life – especially as a boxer.

I turned up one afternoon to take on the might of the Commonwealth pool. Got the trunks on, had a dip to acclimatise myself to the water. Out I got and I stood at the end. You would think I thought I was a world-class diver or swimmer to see me. Standing there concentrating with my toes curled over the tiled edge. But all it was, was me trying to better my underwater swimming record. Nobody was taking any notice of me, thank God. It was me versus the vast stretch of blue out in front. Big breath in and hup! Splash – in I went. I went down and down with the water pressing hard against my ears. I swam along using the breaststroke – that is the best one for underwater, I think. Stroke after stroke I moved up the pool. All I could see was that blue blur and the lines on the bottom all broken and squiggly. And the noise of people screaming, jumping and diving. And every now and then the shrill cry of a lifeguard's whistle. My chest was hard as rocks trying not to breathe, trying not to give in. On and on I went. It seemed forever. There were times when I thought I had lost my bearings and had swam off at a curve. So that I thought I was going in some kind of circle. But then I could see the end – like a pile of broken tiles out there in front. And I knew I was at the shallow end because there were people moving back and forwards, legs and bellies. I gave an extra kick and touched the wall. I burst through the surface and took a big breath. A long, gasping breath. At the same time I had my knuckles in my eyes clearing the water out of them. When I cleared my eyes two old guys were staring at me. I must have looked like I'd just swum up from the centre of the earth, but I had done it.

I'd swim the whole length regularly. It got easier every time. I eventually got to the stage where I could reach the shallow end and turn – giving myself a kick on the wall and propel myself back towards the deep end before surfacing. I never got to do that but I know that training was one of the reasons I never had breathing problems during fights. And besides that, swimming is said to be the best all round exercise you can do. Moving your muscles with the weight taken off them can only do you good.

But back to the Catskill Mountains. After two weeks of intensive training at Grossingers I packed my bags and headed for New York. I was all set to defend my undisputed two titles: the WBC and the WBA lightweight titles. You think you have thought it all out, and you have left nothing to chance. Nothing can possibly go wrong between now and going in the ring. Once you're in there it is all up to you. You're there to show the world what you're made of. I headed for New York prepared for all eventualities. Aye! Wanna bet? Some people will go to any length to give their man the edge.

I settled into my New York hotel. The routine was the same as usual. Then, the night before the fight, I was just settling into bed when I could hear somebody shuffling about outside the door. Voices and somebody walking away, but I knew there was still somebody standing there. The last thing you want to do the night before the fight is get into any fight at all, so I decided to ignore it. But the door goes. A light tap tap tapping. And it's not for stopping. *Who the hell is that?* I thought. My dad had told reception that all callers were to be directed to him – not to disturb me on any account. And sometimes when you're just nodding off – especially the night before a fight – once you get woke up you can't get back to sleep again.

I go to the door, not too pleased. There's a look on my face that would tell you you have two seconds to get lost or else. But when I opened the door there is this beautiful girl. Men's faces are automatic. This big smile floats across my face more gracefully than Ali. She is about nineteen and stunning. A body that is just out of the shop and she is in a baby-doll nightdress. There was flesh everywhere. Legs – thighs – arms – neck – cleavage – all the things I did not want to be thinking about the night before a fight. No, sir. You give up sex for weeks before a fight. So I didn't have to imagine what she was up to as she batted the eyelids and said, 'Are you Ken Buchanan?'

It was like something out of a film. She told me she had been sent to see that I sleep OK. And her eyes gave me that – *If you know what I mean* – look! Boy I have got to say that for a second I was tempted. I mean, who wouldn't be? We're all human, right? My legs were already moving backwards to invite her into the room. But luckily my head was looking after me. It told my mouth to open and say these words; 'Oh, right! I'm not Ken Buchanan – he is in there,' I said pointing to the room next door. It was Eddie's. He was in there with some of his family. His wife's sister or something was there with her husband. I went over and knocked. The girl, in a really professional manner, ignored me, readjusted herself and got ready to do the same routine on the real Ken Buchanan when he came to the door. But it was Eddie's wife's sister who opened up. I pushed the girl forward and said – 'Here's Eddie's hot-water bottle!'

The last thing I saw was the baby-doll slipping into the room as the door closed. I laughed, thankful that my head had over-ruled my body on this one. I put that down to the strict training because – as any boxer knows – you are training your head just as much as you are training your body. Almost as soon as I got into my room, I heard a loud shouting as Eddie tried to explain away his situation. Can you imagine how he got out of that one? Some half-naked babe turning up late at night. And his wife's sister and her husband there? Whoa!

As usual the weigh-in went OK. I was fit. I was focused. Nothing was going to stop me defeating Laguna for the second time. The Scots American Club was there, in the full regalia, to pipe me into the ring. Two American Scots pipers. Boy, did that get my blood going. I was a true Scotsman that night. I didn't care that I couldn't defend my title in Scotland. As far as I was concerned a little piece of Scotland was here to show what us Scots were made of. And it wasn't haggis and tatties and neeps. The atmosphere was electric as we marched towards the ring. Laguna was already in the ring jumping about showing the public he was in good nick for the fight. Throwing a few jabs and hooks.

I climbed in and immediately went over to his corner and shook his hand. I wished him good luck. He tried to say something back but no words came out. He looked rather bemused.

And before I spun away to trot to my own corner I could see his eyebrows looking like they were trying to meet each other in the centre of his forehead. What was I up to? That's what he was thinking. It was obvious that had never happened to him before. But what was I up to? It was all part of the game. You don't need to growl to psyche somebody up. Sometimes all it takes is a friendly hand and a wink. I mean, that could mean anything. Your opponent could spend the whole early part of the fight worrying about what it all means. They'd think you were that cocky you just had to have something up your cuff.

The tale of the tape is a list of all the statistics of us two boxers. But it's interesting to look at. Here's the tale of the tape for the Laguna fight:

World Lightweight Championship
Held in Madison Square Garden
Tale of the Tape

Ken Buchanan, Champion		Ismael Laguna Challenger
26 years	Age	28 years
135 pounds	Weight	135 pounds
5ft 8 inches	Height	5ft 9 inches
71 inches	Reach	70 inches
38 inches	Chest (normal)	36 inches
40 inches	Chest (expanded)	40 inches
29 inches	Waist	28 inches
20 inches	Biceps	19 inches
15½ inches	Neck	15½ inches
14 inches	Calf	13 inches
17 inches	Thigh	18 inches
15 inches	Fist	17 inches
12 inches	Wrist	12 inches
14 inches	Ankle	12 inches

Ding ding – the bell rings for the first round and we get it together. *Jab and move – jab and move Ken*, I say to myself. *Jab and move – keep looking for that opening to throw a right cross.*

I am scoring points and moving – always on the lookout for that opening where I can get in a good combination or a big punch. If that is not going to happen it doesn't matter because I aim to keep scoring and try to win every round. That is what I am doing when the opening comes in the middle of the second round. I have tipped Laguna's head back slightly with a fast jab and it's on its way back into position when – bang! My right cross catches him full on. I felt the shock of it run all the way up my arm to my shoulder. I knew it was a good punch. Laguna's eyebrows are more surprised now than when I shook his hand at the beginning. He takes a breath and tightens up because now he knows he is in for a rough night. I've shaken him, that is for sure. He doesn't seem so sure of himself. Not as steady as he was. About a minute to go in that round and Laguna flicks out a left jab. I lean away from it but I'm not quick enough and the thumb of his glove goes right in my eye. I shake my head and Laguna throws over a snappy right. The right catches me on my left eye and I feel it closing immediately. Ding ding – the bell goes for the end of round-three. My eye has swollen right up – I can feel it. It was clear that Laguna's here to take his title back. I rush to my corner where Eddie tells me to hang on to the ropes. He is going to slit the lump under my eye to release the blood. There is no time to think in the ring – even at the breaks. I do as he says and he gets a razor-blade out. I have only done three rounds and I am not fully warmed up, so the slicing of the eye is painful. Sharp. You have seen it on the *Rocky* film – when Rocky's trainer slits a swelling over his eye. Well, I have it from a good source that they wrote that scene based on this fight, but I'll tell you this – it was hardly Hollywood. Eddie runs the edge of a razor-blade along the cut and the blood comes spurting out.

'Fuck me, Eddie that was sore,' I said. 'Whose side are you on?'

Eddie looks me right in the eyes. 'The swelling's come down a bit so you'll have a few more rounds before it closes.'

I look at him. He holds my head with both his hands and looks right in my eyes. 'You've only got a few more rounds with this eye – do you understand?'

I shook my head. I understood all right. My title was on the line here. The thing is – when I went back to my corner at the end of the second round there was no blood on my face. As far as everybody else was concerned it was the end of a round and there had been no serious injury to either boxer, only a massive swelling under my eye. But when I went out for the start of the fourth there was blood running down my face from where Eddie cut me – right down my cheek. In the mayhem that is a boxing ring I could hear the TV commentator announcing that Buchanan was coming out for the fourth with blood running down his face. He was wondering when that had happened, talking to his pal about it.

It might sound a bit barbaric, but Eddie had done a marvellous job on me. He had given me a couple of extra rounds. If he hadn't done that the fight most certainly would have been stopped – there is no doubt about that. So instead of my left eye being closed going into the fourth, he had bought me some time. The referee would have seen the lump and stepped in. I just wonder how many men in Eddie's position would have done the same? I might not have been getting on with him over money but he was all the man he needed to be for me that day. Good man, Eddie.

The fight goes on. I can see Laguna focusing on that cut. That is all he is thinking about. Open up the cut and get the fight stopped. And why not? That is exactly what I'd be doing. Thank God, my vision isn't too badly affected. But every now and then, Laguna catches it with a jab or sometimes a right. So by the seventh round my left eye finally closes down. When it's like that you can't see a thing coming in from the left – especially right hooks. I have to keep my left up there all the time, and that's no good for my style. It takes that extra fraction of a second to throw a jab and get my hand back up beside my face to protect my eye. And there is no way Laguna doesn't know what is going on with me. He wouldn't be the world-class boxer he is if he doesn't.

So I am now effectively boxing with one eye; Laguna smells victory. At the same time – as the fight goes on I sense that I am in front on points. The body shots I hit Laguna with in the early rounds seem to be paying off. I know I have weakened him. Even though he thinks he can win, he is throwing punches with nothing behind them. I keep taking the fight to him. I know my aggression will wear him down. And it keeps him away from my left eye if I am on the attack. As we go into the last couple of rounds my dad tells me to keep pushing Laguna back with left jabs and right-handers. That is what I do. It keeps him back-pedalling and he can't get a grip with his feet to throw decent punches with any power. It takes some effort and precision to throw a good hard punch while you're moving backwards.

Ding, ding, ding the bell goes to sound the end of fifteen rounds. Was I glad when I heard that. The fight was over. I knew I had done enough to win. But I also knew that if it wasn't for Eddie's quick thinking, I would have lost. The three judges vote in favour of me. I am still undisputed world champion – I have retained my two world titles in America. The feeling is impossible to explain.

Now everybody's running about the ring – my dad hugging me, people saying things I can't hear, me being lifted up . . . but I'm remembering the young Ken. The cold mornings when I'd go out running while my school pals were tucked up in bed. Except for the milk boys and paper boys – at least they were getting paid for what they done. Zoom, zoom, zoom all the images were coming to me. They say a man's life flashes before him when he is dying. It does the same at the pinnacle of your life, too. My life anyway. All the nights in British, European and American gyms flashed up. They were all worth it. That is what the images were saying to me. Give yourself a pat on the back, Ken. You have done well, son. You sacrificed most of your youth, but here you are – top of the world.

The images were right: I'd achieved my life-long ambition. But I'd been living my life on a physical and mental plane far, far removed from normal life. I never had a youth like everybody else. But now was the time to be paid for that sacrifice. All I wanted to do now was get home, to see my son, Mark, hold him in my arms, to be with my family. I only wanted to do the simple things that everybody else takes for granted: relax in front of the television with my feet up drinking cups of coffee. My wife came up to the ring and hugged me. I told her all I wanted to do was go home. She felt the same. When the place cleared a bit she realised she had left the expensive coat I'd bought her in New York a couple days before the fight on her seat. When she went to get it she found somebody had stolen it. You can't trust anybody.

In the hotel getting packed to go home all the razzamatazz of the previous night was still with me. I felt good but very sore all over. And the injuries were starting to nip and throb. I had a few cuts but the worst by far was the one below my left eye – the one Eddie had cut to let the blood out. That was so bad it had needed four stitches inside to pull the gash together. Then the doctor had put in six stitches to pull the skin outside together. I thought nothing of it. Even though it was a bad cut it wasn't the first time I had been sewn up after a fight. And it wouldn't be the last.

Off we went – back home to a life of leisure, telly watching, and a few games of golf – that would be good. But after a couple of days, I started to get some pain from the cut, over and above the normal amount. It was painful if I put any pressure on it. Much the same as a toothache – only much bigger.

I put it down to it being a really bad cut. And it had taken a pounding for quite a few rounds after it had been cut. So after a week the stitches were removed, but my doctor was not very

A busload of supporters came down to London from the Sparta to cheer me on as I beat Jimmy Isaac on points to win the ABA British featherweight title (*Hulton Getty*)

The European championships: winning in Berlin in 1965, just before I decided to turn professional (*Popperfoto*)

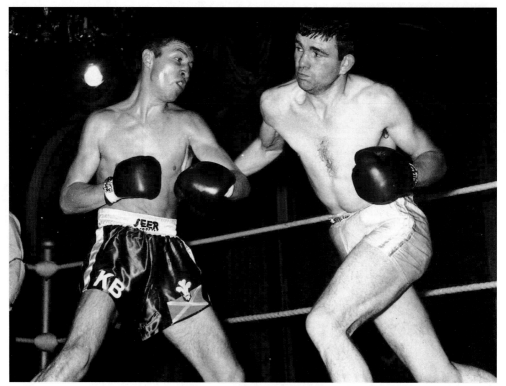

My win against Spike McCormack in 1967 earned me the right to challenge Maurice Cullen for the British lightweight title – it was my hardest fight to date (*Popperfoto*)

In 1968 I was introduced to HRH The Duke of Edinburgh when he attended a boxing dinner at the Anglo American Sporting Club. Heavyweight champion Henry Cooper is on the far right (*PA*)

The next step: Maurice Cullen was betrayed by his smile and I knocked him out in the eleventh round to take the British title (*PA*)

With my manager Eddie Thomas in 1969: he helped me in my early days, but sadly we were to fall out later (*PA*)

My fight against Carlos Hernandez at Wembley in 1971 was only a warm-up until I was able to defend my world title in a rematch against Ismael Laguna in New York (*Popperfoto*)

Returning to the UK with my wife Carol. My eye shows the results of a pounding from Laguna in our rematch, and from Eddie Thomas's cut that enabled me to fight on and retain my world title
(*Popperfoto*)

Proudly wearing my world title belt – all I ever wanted to be was the best in the world.

Leading the dancing with Princess Anne when we were voted Sportswoman and Sportsman of the Year in 1971
(*Popperfoto*)

A very special day: I had yet another brush with royalty when Carol and I went to Buckingham Palace to receive my MBE from the Queen Mother (*PA*)

In 1972, Roberto 'Hands of Stone' Duran stole my world title from me with a late and low punch; a decision which still makes me angry (*Popperfoto*)

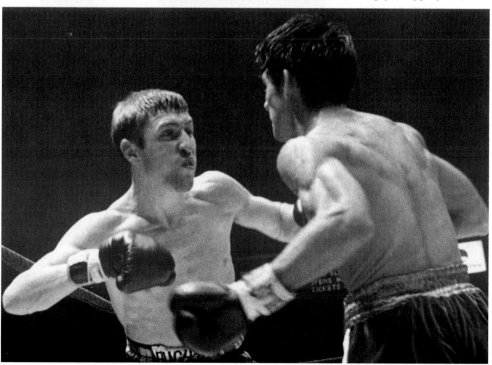

A confident pose, but my dark glasses hide a painful left eye which was badly injured by my sparring partner two days before my world title fight against Guts Ishimatsu in Japan in 1975 (*Popperfoto*)

I boxed well, even with restricted vision, but in the end the decision went against me (*Popperfoto*)

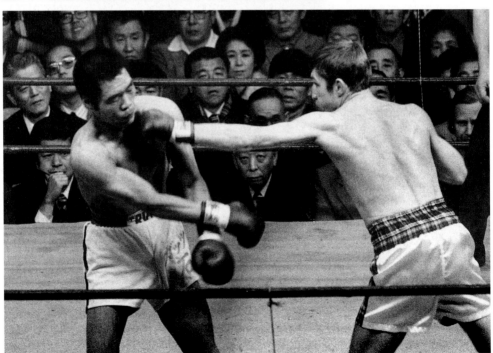

In 1975 I successfully defended my European title against Giancarlo Usai in Italy, but all hell broke loose after the fight and my dad was injured. Here, my son Mark and I check out his stitches (*PA*)

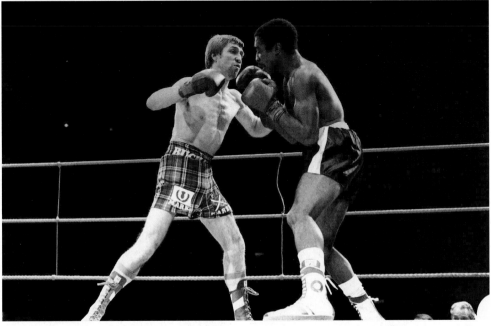

One of my last fights, against Lance Williams in November 1981. Shortly afterwards I decided to hang up my gloves for good (*Popperfoto*)

In 2000, I heard I was to be inducted into the International Boxing Hall of Fame in America. I was given a great Scottish send-off at Glasgow Airport (*PA*)

Meeting Mike Tyson ahead of his fight in Glasgow in the summer of 2000 – a year when so much went well for me

happy about the swelling around my eye. He told me it should be going down and to keep an eye on it (he never even got the joke) and report to him if there was any change. A couple of days pass and I am a guest at the World Sporting Club in London – run by Jack Solomons. As the evening goes on, I am getting pain from my left eye. Near the end of the night the scar started seeping. I went to the toilet and it didn't look good, so Jarvis Astaire recommended me to a Doctor Wallace in Harley Street. He immediately realised that he had to operate on my eye as soon as possible as there was something inside the cut irritating the wound. That came as a bit of a shock. I went out for a night at a boxing club – I'm not even fighting and I end up at the doctor's. Weird!

I made an appointment to have the work done a couple of days later. When he operated on my eye he found the problem. It turned out the New York doctor hadn't put dissolving stitches on the inside of the cut, just ordinary ones. So watch out if you get banged in the eyes over there in the Big Apple – because they might make a big arse of your eye. I must say Doctor Wallace done a great job. You can hardly see the mark on my eye and that is something considering Eddie slashed it, Laguna banged it for twelve rounds, a New York doctor put the wrong stitches in it and it remained swollen for a week and had to be opened up again.

When I'd got over it all, I told Eddie the doctor that he took me to in New York must have been a horse doctor, or drunk, or blind. Or a drunk, blind horse doctor. With my eye having had so much surgery I couldn't train. It was a strange feeling not running in the mornings and not going to the gym. Half of me was itching to get back into it again and half of me was glad I didn't have to do it. Meanwhile, I had nothing to focus on such as a new fight because my contract with Eddie as my manager had run out. But neither of us spoke about it. Instead, every time we meet it's small talk. Yet the weeks went by, and I began to wonder what I was going to do. Where do we go from here? My eye had healed up and I was getting into some light training. But, niggling away in the back of my head, was what was happening with Eddie. How come he hadn't phoned? I had been that used to focusing on a fight, or an opponent or a date. This open-ended time was no good to me, no good at all. I needed something to go on. Eddie eventually phoned.

'How's the eye coming on?'

'Fine! Except for the fact I am not able to fight till at least the end of March '72, the doctor says.'

But neither of us said anything about what was on our minds.

Although there were fights on the horizon, I was bombarded by offers to be a guest at different dinners down in England. It seemed I had become a household name. Ken Buchanan – world champion boxer and underwater swimmer! It was good to milk the publicity, but I should have got myself an agent at this time. Someone to look after all these engagements. Forget about getting up at six in the morning to go out running in the empty streets. Forget turning up at the gym every night for a two to three hour work-out. To forget for a wee while that I am a boxer – even though that is the reason I am getting invited to all these functions.

Later that year I was awarded the MBE and both Carol and myself went to Buckingham Palace to receive my gong from HRH The Queen Mother. It was something really special that day. I told her how I'd recently danced with her granddaughter, Princess Anne. It was true – here I was once again meeting royalty! The reason was, we'd been awarded the title of Sportsman and Sportswoman of the Year and, as was traditional we had to start the dancing. Anyway, it was obvious that Princess Anne hadn't rushed home to tell her gran about the dance as she clearly didn't know what I was talking about.

I never had any weight problems, apart from that episode with the scales in Madrid. I was always a natural lightweight, so even when I was out of training I didn't put on much weight. Weightwatchers would kill for my secret. But I haven't got a secret.

One morning I got a phone call from Eddie. I hadn't heard from him for a wee while and was beginning to think he had lost interest. He wanted to draw up another manager–boxer contract between us, which would normally be governed by the British Boxing Board of Control. But most of my boxing was done in America or Europe. I had only had one fight in Britain as world champion, and it was unlikely there would be many more.

So I told Eddie we wouldn't need to have a contract if I was going to be doing most of my boxing overseas. He hums and haws about the whole thing. (I am told by friends in other walks of life that managers and agents are often just as vague to them.) So I ended up suggesting that if he wanted a British contract, I'd allow him to take only twenty-five per cent of the purse, whether I was boxing in America, Britain, Europe, Timbuktu! By the silence from his end of the phone I could tell he knew this was my response to the fact he had taken a bigger cut of my two American fights, which was not normal. Even though I was grateful to him for cutting my eye at the ringside, now that we were back talking about money things were tense once more. The matter became even more complicated because Jack Solomons had been picking my fights and doing all the negotiations. The British Boxing Board of Control even asked who was my true manager. And to make matters even worse, my young brother Alan decided that he wanted to turn professional, and asked my dad to apply for a manager's licence, which he did. It got to the press that my dad was going to manage *me*, which was never the case, though Alan did go on to be the Scottish featherweight and then lightweight champion.

So, after some very strained talk, Eddie said he'd think it over and get back to me. I waited. And I waited. I wanted to have everything clear, and down on paper, rather than trusting that he would not take the full, larger amount from my purses in the future. I had to protect myself outside the ring as much as I did inside.

One of my faults is that I have been too trusting. Mr Nice – that's me. I waited weeks on Eddie phoning me back, hoping he'd go for the twenty-five per cent I'd suggested. I got a call all right, but it wasn't from Eddie. It was from one of my pals. He told me there was a story in one of the papers about me and Eddie. I rushed out to get a hold of it. I came to an article with a photo of me winning the title, with Eddie in the background. It said Eddie had finished with me. He was quoted as saying that I ditched him because I didn't need him anymore. I couldn't believe it.

I was very hurt reading that story. None of the men in it were the real men. I was put across as a money-crazy boxer who had ditched his friend and manager now that he was famous. And the fact that there was an article at all went against the grain for Eddie. This wasn't Eddie's way of going about things. We're talking here about the man who had slit my eye and gave me the extra rounds to pound Laguna down. No way was this the Eddie I knew. In the six years I had been with Eddie hardly a cross word had passed between us. I knew somebody must have put him up to this; that had to be the case. Just one phone call from Eddie would have resolved this situation. I had no hard feelings against him. I also felt abandoned. All I had done was try to stand up for myself.

But the sore fact was – I was now my own manager. It would be my job to talk to any promoters who wanted me on their bill. To negotiate the purse and the opponent and the venue. The reality of it all is that a fighter has enough on his plate without having to take care of the money side of things, too. If fights had been hard before, they were about to get a lot harder. It was a quick learning process. I had never questioned Eddie's decisions as to who I should fight – and where – and when. I was about to learn that boxing was about much more than just throwing punches – much more.

unlucky thirteenth

After the break-up with Eddie, the first promoter to contact me was Harry Levene. He wanted me to box Al Ford from Canada at Wembley on 28 March. That would work out at approximately six months since my last fight. Even though the doctor had advised me to stay out of the ring for much longer than that, I took the fight.

Al Ford was a good boxer. He was in the top ten ratings so I had to be careful not to slip up. I was worried about my eye, in case I hadn't given it enough time to knit together properly. A bad pounding could have ended my boxing career forever. I made sure the bout was tagged a non-title fight over ten rounds, and won it comfortably on points. But two things of importance happened that night. One – my left eye never opened up during the fight, and it took some hard knocks. I took a great amount of relief from that. Two – I'd gone through a full ten rounds without Eddie in my corner. And I took a great deal of encouragement from that.

Yet, if I was honest, I'd have to say that I missed Eddie being there. He had been the rock in my corner along with my dad since I turned professional. During the fight there were times when I felt as if there was a gap behind me. Before, when Eddie was there I felt the corner was solid. The corner was somewhere to go back to, a kind of safe haven. Even though I had managed my first fight without Eddie rather well, there was no doubt I was going to miss him. But life has to go on. Even for world champion boxers who have just parted with their manager. And I certainly wasn't going to be sitting about twiddling my thumbs. I had some underwater swimming to do. I had to get as fit as I possibly could to counteract the fact that Eddie wouldn't be in my corner anymore.

I was thinking about a fight in Los Angeles at the time. Eileen Eaton wanted me to defend my title against Jimmy Robertson there. It would have been a good earner, but instead I decided to fight Andries Steyn in Johannesburg at the Rand Stadium. Steyn was an aggressive boxer and his record proved he was no walkover. But I preferred him because he had not fought in the same company as myself. Most of his fights had been in Johannesburg and he'd be a big attraction. That would mean a good purse. I got right into training.

Whether it was to be a world title fight or not I always made sure I was in the best of shape. I arranged to be in South Africa at least ten days before the fight, to get acclimatised. It was hot in South Africa but nowhere near the searing heat of Puerto Rico. My days up to the fight consisted of the usual running in the morning and a couple of hours in the gym at night. Fight day came and, before the weigh-in, the usual questions were answered.

How do you think you'll do Ken? Does it worry you fighting so far from home Ken? How do you rate your opponent Ken?

I stood on the scales which were set at 137 pounds. I knew I was under the weight anyway, my training had gone really well and I felt really fit. The scales stood still. I was under the limit. Steyn's dad shouted that I be weighed out to find exactly how much I weighed. I told him this is a non-title fight. It was made at two pounds over the recognised championship weight. By boxing rules I don't have to be weighed out as long as I am not over 137 pounds. But he wouldn't listen, Mr Steyn. Now I was getting a bit pissed off. He was doing his best to upset me before the fight, and he had. But I bit my tongue – held the rage back and said, 'Mr

Steyn, I'd have been quite happy to box your son for ten rounds and win unanimously on points.' I remember his mouth hanging open as the whole place goes silent and they all turn to watch me. I went on, 'But seeing as how you're acting like an arsehole I am going to knock him out as soon as I can.'

Mr Steyn stormed off. Members of the Boxing Board of Control in Johannesburg apologised to me for his outburst. He had been warned never to open his mouth again.

After the weigh-in I went back to the hotel, had a nice steak, baked potato and salad. It feels great to get some good grub inside you after the weigh-in. It energises you for the fight to come. I took a short stroll to work off my dinner. It was a nice sunny day, but not too hot. There was a pleasant atmosphere about the place and I was feeling good. I went back to the hotel for a lie-down till I had to go to the stadium. That combination of a meal and a walk and a rest seemed to always do the trick for me.

The stadium was almost packed. There must have been over ten thousand people watching that night. I think there was a large number of fans from Britain, most of whom were working or having a holiday in South Africa – but some had actually flown over for the fight. Now there's dedication for you. When I entered the ring I was given a tremendous ovation. There were St Andrew's flags and Union Jacks waving everywhere.

It gives a fighter a lift to see he is not there alone. And me being such a proud Scotsman it gave me a great lift to see all the Saltires waving about in that warm breeze.

The first round starts and I move into the centre of the ring and touch gloves with Andries. I move back and start throwing punches. Straight left then jabs again and again. I find as early as the first round Andries does not have a clue what to do with my fast and accurate jab. He is confused by its speed. I continue to get through at him. Ding ding the bell goes to end the round and I go back to my corner – neither up nor down. I hadn't felt threatened the whole round. Not one bit. I mean, he hadn't hit me.

Once I was back and sitting down my dad says, 'Well, son, you looked good in that round. I don't think he landed a decent glove on you.'

'You're right, dad. He's ready for the taking. Did you notice how he drops his left glove every time he forces a right at me?'

'I seen that son. Every time.'

'When he does it next I'll explode my right glove on his chin.'

The second round goes like the first. I'm all over him but just miss knocking him out. The bell goes to end round two. Most of the time the talk in the corner about the tactics for the next round comes to nothing. Usually because whatever you have seen as a weakness in the opponent – so has their corner. Or the fight goes off in another direction. But this time, after two rounds, the talk worked out. I got the chance to force a right through. He jabbed a left and his right hand dropped a bit and in I went. Bang! And that is how the fight finished. In the third round Andries Steyn is counted out. Andries came over to my corner after the bells stopped ringing in his head. He grabbed my hand and lifted it. That was a lovely gesture. And you don't get a lot of them in boxing. He obviously didn't take his manners from his dad's side of the family. Andries works for a radio company now and he often talks about the fight he had with me way back in 1972.

When I got home from South Africa it was like I had been on holiday – not away fighting. The fight had taken nothing out of me and I hadn't been injured at all. I found that my mail had built up quite a bit. Some of the small things give you great pleasure in life. That was one of the things I liked – coming home and a pile of letters waiting to be opened. I always thought there was going to be one there saying: Dear Ken, we want to give you a million pounds to fight so and so. But that never happened. If only I was fighting in this day and age . . .

There was a very interesting letter waiting for me, with an American stamp on it. I kept that till the end. It looked like the best letter. And I was right. It was from Madison Square Garden and they were offering me a lot of money to fight. OK, it was not a million, but it felt like it. They were offering $100,000 for me to fight Roberto Duran at Madison Square Garden on 26 June 1972.

Even so things got complicated when I was stripped of my WBC title for not taking on the Spanish boxer Pedro Carrasco, who they thought was a more worthy contender than Duran. Carrasco better than Duran! Carrasco had given up the European lightweight title 'cause he could no longer make 135 lbs. One man was struggling to make the weight, while the other was to become one of the all-time greats. There was no question in my mind which fight I had to take.

It was a big purse for a lightweight. After tossing and turning for about two seconds, I phoned my dad and told him I was going to take the fight with Duran. I had to or the WBA would have stripped me of my title. Little did I know what it was leading to. A moment that would haunt me forever. Even to this day as I am writing this book I can't get what happened at that fight out of my head. As usual I trained hard for several weeks, then I flew off to New York where I completed my training for the fight at Grossingers. I decided to get Gil Clancy the manager and trainer of Emile Griffith to work in my camp, as he was a well-respected guy. Gil organised the sparring partners for me. The rest I took care of: running and resting and eating like I always did.

Gil had taken two sparring partners up to Grossingers. But after a couple of days they both wanted to go home; they said I was too hard on them. The way I saw it I was paying them good money so I was entitled to my pound of flesh. Gil asked me to go a little bit easier on them. He said he couldn't get hold of anybody else at such short notice. I wasn't too pleased about it but I had to pull back my punches in sparring. As I have said before, nobody in sparring is trying to take your head off. I was just training as hard as I would for any fight. Maybe the aggression over the Eddie affair was coming out, but honestly, as far as I was concerned I was just my normal self in sparring. To compensate for not being able to hit hard in sparring, when I got on the heavy bag I hit it as hard as I could. I got so much out of that I decided to cut my sparring down and work more on the heavy bag. Had I done more work than usual on the hand pads which my dad held for me. In the end, it turned out that the sparring partners were getting paid for almost nothing.

Time flashes past and we're finished there before we know it. The training is over, I am honed as much as I possibly could be and we all head back to New York the day before the fight. As usual I was raring to get in there and show the world what I could do.

For more than one reason. Everybody knows that fighters have to stay away from their wives prior to a fight, for a full three weeks usually. It is all part of the training regime. Well, I had done all that as usual. Funny thing is – after the first couple of weeks sex-free, it stops bothering you. I mean you still think about it but it's not as intense. The fight takes over your every minute, every waking thought.

During the fight I thought I wasn't as snappy as I should have been. It was probably all in my mind. And that was the problem: it *was* all in my mind. And it shouldn't have been. I felt that my body was somehow different. That I was doing things I shouldn't have been doing in the ring. I just didn't feel right in myself. When you're training you're like a monk. Everything is regimented: food, training, sleep. You can't let anything interfere with it. I decided in the ring that I was going to retire if I won that fight with Duran. I had made enough money: $100,000 was not a real fortune, but enough to retire on. I was looking to go into business. I still had my head and my brains intact, I think. At the weigh-in Duran was so cocky it bored me. We weighed out and the doctor passed both of us as fit to fight.

The night of the fight goes along as normal. My hands are taped and the Vaseline is on my body. The tartan boxing pants are on, shorts which were made for me personally by Mrs Carr from

Edinburgh. I got a tremendous reception when I entered the ring from the American and British fans who were kitted out in kilts and flags. These were the fans I had built up since my first appearance way back in December 1970 when I first topped Madison Square Garden.

Madison Square Garden. Here I was in New York defending my world lightweight title against a man who was on his way to becoming a legend. A man from Colón, Panama – the very same place where Ismael Laguna came from. Roberto 'Hands of Stone' Duran. They don't half think up some daft names for boxers. I am glad they never thought up one for me. Knowing what we all know now – that Duran went on to win world titles at four different weights – it would be obvious that this was going to be no ordinary fight. There was a headier atmosphere than usual. You become some kind of strange barometer for measuring atmosphere and this was right up there bending the needle. Duran was out to win no matter what the consequences. You could see that on his eager face. And boy did I find that out.

The bagpipes are playing away in front of me and the many Scottish immigrants are screaming their heads off for me. When the bell goes for the first round Duran comes rushing out of his corner throwing left and rights. He is like a wild animal released from a cage. I think he thinks he is going to finish me off and go home for his tea. Well – as eager as he is – I am here to keep my title. Maybe a couple of his punches land and I retaliate with a couple of left jabs to his face. I could tell he was surprised by the speed of my jabs. This was the way the fight went. Him coming at me and me retaliating by jabbing and moving. Coming in with combinations whenever he left himself open. An opponent can only fight as well as you allow him to. That is true, apart from when the referee is on his side. The referee later said he thought he had let Duran get away with too much. That was the feeling I was getting as the fight went on. You get a gut feeling for a fight – even before you step in the ring. I realised this was going to be a hard one.

Duran was rushing and pushing me about the ring and getting away with it. For a minute I thought I signed up for a wrestling match and not a boxing contest. Duran hits me up the balls a couple of times without so much as a warning from the referee. Not even a nod. And it's fuckin' sore, I can tell you that. With the referee missing things like that there is not much I can do to stop this apart from making him miss and countering with a jab. Avoiding him and countering is what I will have to do the whole fight.

At the end of the eleventh I feel that we are about even on points. Roberto has thrown more punches than me, but has also missed with a lot. The twelfth round has Duran coming on to me, but by this time I have got the makings of him. As he comes forwards I just flick out jabs at his head. Scoring all the time while he is not scoring at all. You can tell it's making him mad. He feels his chance at the world title slipping away from him. The bell goes and I retire to my corner for a rest. At this time of the fight I don't have a mark on my face. The punches Duran threw have not marked me in any way. I don't even have a nosebleed. He, on the other hand, is dripping blood from the mouth and his nose is busted. My constant picking away at him has produced results.

As the thirteenth round gets underway I find myself catching Duran with my right hand over the top of his left jab. I'm catching him more and that's when I realise he is tiring. I was still feeling good. We were nearing the end of the thirteenth and I let go with a left–right combination which hits Duran lightly. He just shrugs them off thinking that is all I have and comes at me again. I throw the same combination again. This time I hurt him. His eyes roll up and back down again. I let go with another left–right – catching him on the head. It rocks him. His hands are going down. If the round goes on for another thirty seconds I will stop Duran. He knows it; I know it. And we're the only people who need to know it.

The bell goes. I ease up – you un-tighten at the sound of the bell, automatically – right off my guard as I turn towards my corner. In the same moment Duran lunges up from the floor with a punch that went right into my balls, pushing my protector into my groin. Oh what a fuckin' pain there is down there. A roar goes up from the crowd. I'm on my knees, down, but the referee does not count 'cause he knows the punch was thrown after the bell. Now I know why they call him 'Fists of Stone'. It's the worst thing ever! Gil Clancy and my dad jump in the ring and help me get back to my corner. You can imagine the confusion in the ring.

I now put out a challenge to the boxing world – just as verdicts in courtrooms are overturned years later with the right evidence – I think the boxing powers-that-be should watch the video of that fight and award the fight – even at this late date – to me. By the way – if they do – I am retiring as the champion – so no challengers please.

There was madness all around me. Voices were coming and going, like somebody was turning the volume up and down. Faces were zooming in and out of my view. 'Are you able to continue Ken? Where exactly does it hurt? Where's your gum-shield?'

I sat on my stool. My dad asks how I am. I remember asking what round it was, but there was so much shouting and arguing nobody could be heard. I didn't know what was going on. But there was something happening in the middle of the ring. Nobody even came over to see me.

Then, before I could get myself together, there was Duran jumping about in the ring. Lobianco the referee has lifted Duran's hand. How could he have done that without asking me if I wanted to continue? It should have been me who was awarded the fight. That was the last thing I saw as I was being helped out of the ring. And – as I have said – those few minutes were to haunt me all my life. Everybody about me was seething with anger. The whole place knew I was robbed. The arena was buzzing. Booing. They couldn't believe how the fight had ended. Tony Lobianco was saying nothing. He was trying to get away with a few heavies round about him keeping the crowd at bay. He knew he was going to get lynched. He was off, marching out of the arena with people chasing him like barking dogs. That fight was his first go at refereeing a world title – and his last. He never refereed a fight at that level again. It seems the whole world agreed with me that Duran was wrongly awarded the contest. But who was prepared to do something about it? Nobody – that's who!

I look back as I stumble towards the dressing-rooms. The ring is invaded with people. I am helped back into the dressing-room. I take off my pants. You can see the mark on my protector where it's been hit several times. My balls are turning red, swelling up.

My dad and I went to the official from the New York State Boxing Commission. He said he couldn't understand why Duran hadn't been disqualified for that low blow as, not only had Duran hit me in the balls, he had – there was no dispute about this – hit me after the bell. They were not interested in the punch being after the bell. As for the low blow being the one that caused me not to be able to fight on, my dad was told that the New York State Boxing Commission did not accept that a fighter wearing a protector could be hurt. But my dad had anticipated this and whipped the protector out of his pocket. He asked the President to put my protector on and he'd hit him on the balls. Then he could say that he did not accept that a boxer wearing a protector could not be hurt. But Mr Dooley could not be persuaded to take part in the experiment. I also told him I could produce a photo of Henry Cooper writhing on the canvas in agony after a low blow, and there were others who had been similarly caught.

Then there was Phil Scott. He was the man who had twice claimed a victory in Madison Square Garden because of an alleged low blow. Hence the New York State Boxing Commission passed the rule that a fight could not be won on a low blow. 'Phainting' was the nickname the Americans gave to Phil Scott as he fought only twice in Madison Square Garden and each time he lay down on the canvas claiming to have been hit by a low blow. I don't think protectors were worn in those days – but it is possible Phil Scott made a case for them. I have been hit low in lots of fights, but the only one I went down in was the Duran fight.

It was no consolation the following day when Tony Lobianco was at the television studios watching a rerun of the fight that he admitted the punch was after the bell and under my waist. But he said he made his decision on the spur of the moment like any normal referee. He could have just as easily disqualified Duran on the spur of the moment, but he didn't.

They said the result could not be changed. You can't change the past. But I'll tell you something – you can change the future. I had a contract for a return fight against Duran in three months, so at least I know what I would be up against. In my mind I was going to pound him into the ground. I was going to be in peak condition, fitter than I had ever been, harder than ever. Duran would see what it is like to be in with a boxer. And I would be more equipped when we fight again, wearing a cast-iron protector and a big sign that says: WAIST. NO SHOTS BELOW THIS LEVEL.

bring on duran

But Duran would never go back in the same ring as me – and that hurt more than the bad decision. To this day I still get pains in my groin. I should have put a claim in for criminal injuries. Even up to this day Duran has never boxed again in Madison Square Garden. But he is a good shot, I'll give him that. Right on the button he caught me. If Roberto Duran was a darts player he could hit the bull dead on every time. The thing about the fight was that apart from the low punch in the thirteenth round, Duran never badly hurt me. I had had much harder fights in my time.

That one late blow went a long way to destroying my career. It was the turning point of my life. I never knew it then – but that is what it was to turn out to be. I only wanted to be the world champion for a few years and then retire undefeated. I didn't want to keep going and end up some bum that used to be a champ but was now boxing just for the cash. But when the Duran thing happened I had to keep fighting. I had no other choice. People said I did it only for the money – well what else would I do it for? Bus tokens? I couldn't do anything else. My whole life had been geared towards boxing. Every thought and movement.

On coming back to Edinburgh I visited my doctor who sent me to the hospital for ten days. To put it politely – my balls were killing me. I was walking like John Wayne. I was pissing blood. I'll tell you this – it was a pretty scary time. I had to hold my balls in my hand when I wanted to walk anywhere. That's something for a boxer who can't be hurt when he is wearing a protector. And every time the shock of pain ran through my body all I could think about was getting back in the ring with Duran and pounding him down round after round. In the end the doctors explained that a vein had been damaged in my balls. They were unable to operate and I was told they would always be painful.

As the weeks fly past I was constantly on the phone to Teddy Brenner at Madison Square Garden. I wanted to know when the return fight with Duran would take place. I was dying to get back in the ring with him and give him a good hiding. I have never wanted anything so much in all my life. I would have fought him on the back streets of Harlem if he gave me half the chance. But Teddy Brenner has not got any good news for me. He tells me Duran wants to take a non-title fight in Panama then he'll defend the title against me. *When?* I want to know. Around Christmas is the answer. Teddy Brenner gives me his word that I'll get my crack at Duran. So it was going to be a merry Christmas for me, but there would be nothing coming from Santa that year for Duran.

In the meantime I got back to the gym. I had to work out very lightly. The bruising around my sore balls was getting better. Eventually I built up the pace. I sparred with a lot of the amateurs and did some boxing exhibitions at amateur shows up and down the country. I was getting better and fitter, I was pacing my fitness this time. I want to hit peak condition at Christmas. My whole life was aiming at the end of the year and Duran's grinning face.

Then one night I got a phone call from Madison Square Garden – Teddy Brenner again. He wanted to know if I would fight Carlos Ortiz in Madison Square Garden on 20 September. I asked about my old pal Duran. He told me Duran had pulled a muscle in training, and couldn't fight Ortiz. Would I stand in? I thought for a minute then said yes to the Carlos Ortiz fight. If Duran had been meant to fight him, then this was a step towards Duran for me. And a fight about now would be good for my fitness and confidence. Don't get me wrong – he was no pushover,

Ortiz. He had been a great world champion at lightweight and light welterweight. He had made a recent comeback and had a string of wins at welterweight. He had had ten comeback fights and won them all. Nine knockouts and one on points.

The fight was to be on the same card as Muhammad Ali and Floyd Patterson. I'd be giving away about a stone in weight to Ortiz. But I knew if I moved around there fast enough I could tire him out.

I worked hard as usual to build up to the fight. I knew Carlos had a good right hand so I wasn't going to take any chances, and I'd stay well out the road of it. I flew over to New York with my dad and met up with Gil Clancy in the hotel outside Madison Square Garden. We had a good chat, mostly about Ortiz, then went for dinner. I finished the night off with a walk round the streets of New York. I was a speck moving along at the bottom of the gigantic buildings. It was brilliant – I wished some of my pals could see me then.

The next day at the weigh-in the place was jam-packed with reporters and photographers and all sorts of people. They were still asking me about the Duran fight on top of the questions about this fight with Ortiz. I gave them the same answers to all the Duran questions. Which boiled down to – *Where is he? Bring him on.* Dooley, President of the New York State Boxing Commission, was presiding over the weigh-in. When it was his turn to be weighed in, Ortiz put his hand on Dooley's shoulder. Dooley seemed unaware of this and was surprised when my dad asked him to re-weigh Ortiz.

The place was buzzing. There was always plenty of buzz when Ali was about. After we all weighed in and were passed by the doctor I went out to lunch with my dad, Gil and my aunt Joan and uncle George from Toronto, who had flown down the day before the fight.

When fight time came round it was the same routine in the dressing-room. Clancy would put my bandages on, my dad would smother me in Vaseline. There were twenty thousand people out there waiting. My plan was to use my speed and tire Ortiz down for the first six rounds, while staying clear of his punches. A hard punch is one thing – but a hard punch from a man who is a stone heavier is another thing again. I would hit and run for six rounds. If his strength was failing then – I'd go in for the kill. And that is just the way it happened. Only much earlier. Ortiz seemed to be weakening at the end of the third so I switched to attack then. I went for him all through the fourth and fifth rounds. He was very slow off his stool for the sixth round and I knew it would all be over soon after. I had hurt him in the fourth and fifth, especially with shots to the body. He was getting what Duran should have got. All during that fight the realisation that I was fighting in Madison Square Garden stayed tucked away in my head. I had fought in the USA five times now – and to me it was like fighting at home. Bring on Duran was all I could say to myself. Bring on Duran.

Before leaving New York, Teddy Brenner asked me if I was doing anything at the beginning of December. My heart started beating. Yes – here it is – the offer of the return fight with Duran at last. But it wasn't Duran, so did I still want to fight? Yes.

So that was me: ready for another fight at the Gardens, waiting to find out who my opponent would be. I went back home and kept in good shape. Teddy phoned the middle of November with the news that I was to fight Chang Kil Lee a light welter-weight from Korea. Lee was three inches taller than me and six pounds heavier. I liked fighting taller men so I agreed to the match. Lee had only had twenty-two fights but was the undefeated Korean champion. He had got good credentials, so I had to take care. When I eventually met Lee in New York he was everything I thought he'd be.

I go through the same routine again and, before you know it, it's fight time. In the first round I get my measure of Lee. Because he is taller than me he holds his hands possibly further down his chest than he would normally, probably thinking I'd find it hard to get shots in at his head. The first round goes by OK. I am scoring well with my good body shots and straight lefts to the face. Back in the corner my dad tells me to jab his face for about a minute then drop the big right on to his chin.

A minute into the second round I throw a light left jab. It just catches his face – I drop the big right hand as I am pulling the jab back. Every little movement of my body is perfect. My feet are in solid contact with the floor. My waist swivels just the right amount to get maximum power behind the blow. Bang! – Lee is on the canvas. His eyes are rolling about. The count goes to six and Lee gets to his feet, but he is wobbling all over the place. His brain might be back on board but his body isn't yet responding to his commands. I sense the end is coming up. I go forward with a barrage of lefts and rights. Lee is in bad trouble trying to cover up but it's no good. I am getting through with almost everything. Even though you know your opponent is in a bad position you can't let him off the hook. You have to keep going until the referee decides it is time to stop the fight. Every boxer knows and accepts that. The referee jumps between us and calls a halt to the fight. Yes! Another win in my wait for the Duran fight. Surely he can't keep hiding from me now. I am sending out a clear message to him.

I hinted to Teddy Brenner that this was my second fight in New York since I fought Duran, but the Gardens still didn't have a date for a rematch. I went home happy with the win and the purse, but not too chuffed about the uncertainty over Duran. I knew I had to keep fighting so as not to get rusty.

About a week before Christmas and I got a call from Les Roberts, the matchmaker for the National Sporting Club in London. He told me he was opening a similar sporting club in Glasgow at the end of January '73. Would I like to fight Jim Watt for the British lightweight title? I decided to take it on.

I got to thinking about this fight: if I beat Jim Watt I would keep the Lonsdale Belt. I had always wanted one of those for myself. I already have two notches for beating Maurice Cullen and Brian Hudson. Once you had three you got to keep it. The news of the fight had filtered through to the press. As expected, there was a lot of hot air flying about. The ex-world champion challenging Jim Watt for the British title in Glasgow. It had been a long time since there had been such a big fight in Scotland. So the slagging match started. OK, we all do a bit of mouthing off to the press, that's the name of the game. But when you get down to the bottom line Jim and me are really fighting to see who is the better boxer. That is all there is to it. As I said, once you climb in that ring all you have is your ability to show the world who you are. No amount of mouthing and bragging is going to make you a better man on the day.

In the build-up Jim's manager, Jim Murray, continually slagged me in the papers. He was saying that I was well past my best, and that I couldn't walk and chew gum at the same time. He sent a letter to the press saying that they should have a stretcher at the ringside for me. That was really bad. It can make you angry all that slagging, but the one about the gum and walking, I actually found quite funny. If anything, my co-ordination was bang on. I had to laugh – couldn't walk and chew gum at the same time. Headcase!

At this time I was managing myself. So I had to do the talking to the media that a manager would normally do. Even though Jim Watt's manager was laying into me I remained fairly silent in the run-up to the fight, said nothing to the press apart from the usual stuff. I never slagged Jim at all. And I tried hard not to get involved with Jim Murray's antics – although it was hard not to when he was such an easy target. He set himself up for it all the time. I avoided talking about my own ability. One of the problems I had was talking about myself and trying not to sound big-headed. But I think – in my opinion! – I conducted myself well right up to the fight.

They said it was going to be a cracker – and they were right. Fighting Jim for the Lonsdale Belt turned out to be a 'belter'.

When I climbed in the ring I could see the eagerness sparkling in his eyes. And even now I have to give all credit to Jim for putting up a tremendous defence of the title. We were both in there fighting with everything we had. And we both had guts – plenty of them. Not for the want of trying; there was only one point in the fight where I managed to hurt him. Give him his due – he held on to me and didn't let go till the ref told us to break. He recovered very quickly. After that it was back to boxing it out as ferociously as before. Every time he came at me I could see myself when I was twenty-five – out there in Puerto Rico – chasing a dream. It was non-stop from start to finish. To be honest, I think our fight was one of the best Jim ever boxed. I seemed to bring out the best in him. He never gave up, and after fifteen rounds we were both knackered.

At the end of the gruelling contest Jim Watt thought he had done well enough to win, but I felt the exact same. To be fair, I'd been around a wee bit longer than Jim. The simple fact was that he didn't have enough experience for me that night. That is all it was. I knew I had won. When I was announced the new British champion I was over the moon. The Lonsdale Belt was mine for good.

I grabbed the microphone and told the packed hall that I felt, given the chance, Jim could be a world champion one day. And his dream came true against Alfredo Pitalua in Glasgow, in April 1979 when he stopped Pitalua in twelve rounds.

Even though I had won the fight and the Lonsdale Belt outright, I gave up the British title a couple of weeks later. I was still on the lookout for Duran. Or, if I couldn't get him, I was still on the hunt for a world title. I took fights in Miami, New York, Toronto, Copenhagen, Cagliari and Paris – winning all thirteen after the Duran bout. I was on a roll again. I could feel it, but where was Duran?

Instead, I got a call from London asking if I'd like to fight Hector Matta from Boston, on 27 March at the Kensington Sporting Club over ten rounds. It sounded OK to me so I started my preparation. The fight was made at nine stone eleven pounds. Matta wasn't in the world top ten, but I was told he was a spoiler in the ring. I trained with that in mind, but as a boxer who likes to move around the ring I knew that his style would not given me too much bother.

I had to make sure I didn't get caught in the corners or the ropes. I jabbed and moved, jabbed and moved. I was always a boxer first and a fighter second. I relied on keeping cool and on my technical ability. And once again that style proved to be the one for me. I boxed the head off Matta for ten rounds. It was more like a work-out than a regular fight and I won it unanimously. I was keeping fit and in fighting condition and getting a pay day at the same time. Can't be bad. These things happen when one boxer wants to box and the other wants to maul his opponent.

Later I got a call from Chris Dundee, Angelo's brother, wanting to know if I'd be interested in coming over to Miami to fight their local fighter Frankie Otero. He was number eight in the world ratings and was unbeaten in forty fights. We agreed to fight over ten rounds at 137 pounds.

He said he would send me over the contracts to sign. Before I ever signed a contract I always made sure that the name of the guy I was going to fight was written on the contract, especially when the fight was abroad. You never knew what they might do to you on the night.

Then Teddy Brenner rang to ask if I'd like to box in the Gardens on their show in May. Sadly, I had to turn him down as I am obligated to fight for Chris Dundee in Miami. Teddy agreed to put me in on his show on 1 September. The offers just kept on coming, but still no Duran. Where is that guy? I had to put him out of my mind by concentrating on the two fights I had coming up. Two more pay days. I began to think I'd be as well living in America as that was where I seemed to be making all my money, especially as now I was managing myself, my only ties were my wife and son.

In Miami I was met at the airport by Chris Dundee and his driver. He took us to the Fontainbleu Hotel. Man – what a place that was! It was probably the best hotel I had ever been in. It had everything you would want. When you walked out the rear entrance you stepped on to a spectacular beach. They even owned part of the Miami beach – now there's class for you.

Seeing how I had done most of my heavy work in Edinburgh I did some light training for a few days, mostly jogging and light sparring. Long walks along the beach at night were great. I was so relaxed. It's very hot in Miami. I just had to blow my nose and I was sweating, but I still had to keep my head on the job at hand. Frankie Otero was a lightweight and he had a good record. He was on his way up and there was no way he wanted to lose this fight. The fight was a sell-out and there were over seven thousand people packed into the hall. This fight was quoted as an eliminator for the world title fight.

When we are in the ring he is in good condition. I have to take my hat off to him there. He looked as fit as any boxer I had ever seen. I remember thinking that I'd have to be on my toes all of the ten rounds. After a couple of rounds I realise his punches don't hurt me. That doesn't mean to say I let him hit me. He is light on his feet and, like me, good at using the ring. We're similar boxers in some ways. It would have been a good exhibition match if it wasn't for real. After the two of us had been moving all over the ring for a few rounds I decide to claim the centre of the ring, make him do all the running. In my head I am using this fight as a warm-up to my fight in New York a couple of months later. And that is how it ended up. I won on points. But let me tell you what happened in that fight.

Towards the end of the fight, Frankie is getting a little tired. He throws a left jab, I duck it and it goes over my shoulder. Then he just drops his weight on to me. I'm getting tired of this and it's sapping my energy, so I decide to teach him a lesson. The next time he does it, I let him slowly rest his weight on me and I bend my knees slightly so Frankie comes down with me. Once his full weight is on me I come up, quick as a flash, and Frankie goes flying over my shoulder. Unluckily for me, he pulls me down with him and we both collapse into a heap. I catch his eye and we both burst out laughing, which sets off the referee and the crowd. Glad to say nobody was hurt!

At long last I got offered a bout with real meaning, against Rudolpho Gonzales for his WBC world lightweight title. Yes – another world title fight. It might not have been Duran but it would do for now – and it would put me in a position where Duran could hardly refuse to fight me. The fight was to be in Los Angeles on 28 September 1973.

Two days before I was due to go to London to sign the contract for this fight, I was informed that the WBC had decided that Antonio Puddu of Italy was to get this fight with Gonzales instead of me. This was the same WBC who had stripped me of my would title for something they must have known was no fault of mine. Now they were denying me the chance to try for it again. Their reasoning was that as Puddu was the reigning European champion they had to give him his shot at the world title. I was gutted. The next year I was to KO Puddu in Italy for the European lightweight title, which showed I was still the more legitimate challenger. The WBC wanted to be fair to Puddu because they had stopped him fighting Duran for his WBA world lightweight title some weeks before.

It all seemed ridiculous. There must have been outside influences involved in all this. I am not aware that any action was ever taken by the British Boxing Board of Control to defend my claim to that fight with Gonzales, even though they always took a percentage of my purse whenever I fought abroad, and almost all my fights were outside British territory. I was angry that a chance to fight for a world title had been taken out of my hands. And even more angry because that's when I got the feeling that the return with Duran was slipping beyond my control, too. Already it was more than a year since our first bout.

In the end Gonzales stopped Puddu in the tenth round. A week later, Ray Clarke, secretary of the British Boxing Board of Control, attended a meeting of the WBC in Brazil. It was their annual congress and Ray Clarke was there to back the claims of a number of British boxers, me included. It was decided at that meeting that Ken Buchanan was to be recognised as the number one contender for the WBC world lightweight title. Great. I didn't argue with that. There was a buzz. Surely now I couldn't be denied a fight with Gonzales? And yet for the second time I didn't get the fight. Instead, Gonzales ended up fighting Ishimatsu Suzuki from Japan, and he lost. Ishimatsu ended up defending the title twice before he eventually fought me in February 1975. By which time, I think everyone had run out of excuses.

taking on europe

I am back in the Gardens again. Up against a Puerto Rican, Edwin 'Chu Chu' Malave. No wonder he ended up being a boxer with a name like that: choo choo. Every time I heard his name I thought of the Johnny Cash song: 'A Boy Named Sue'. Chu Chu is about five feet ten inches tall and weighs ten stone. He has a fair record and he has been in the ring with a couple of good fighters. This looks like it is going to be a harder fight than I thought. But that would be good in some ways – it would test me at another level.

The fight is hard. Chu Chu is trying to land the big one. I keep well out his road and score points the way I always do. After the fifth round I am slightly ahead on points but Chu Chu is still dangerous. With about thirty seconds of the fifth to go we both throw fast and heavy right hands. But we both miss the target and the momentum carries us forwards. Out heads clash and we're both badly cut above the left eyes. There goes that old left eye again. I have to finish the whole affair, I can see that. I pile up the points with lots of head punches which burst Chu Chu's nose and mouth. He is looking badly hurt when the bell goes. But so am I, it seems, because when I get back to the corner my cut-man Freddie Hill tells me I have only one round left because the cut above the left eye is so bad. 'How bad is it?' I ask him.

'It's like a trout's mouth,' he says.

He should be a poet, Freddie. Freddie can't see the referee allowing the fight to go on, especially when he gets a good look at the cut. All I could think about now was knocking Chu Chu out. I had to knock him out. We got through the next round, but I'll never forget what the referee said to me at the start of the seventh round: 'I can't let this fight go on much – you're both badly cut – there is blood everywhere.'

Referees have said a lot of strange things to me in the past but this one really stunned me. The situation is – I am ahead on points but could lose the fight after this round if it gets stopped. What the referee was actually saying is – I'll give you this round to stop your opponent. If you don't, I will have to stop it.

Both of us are moving around the ring throwing light jabs. Just looking for that opening. That punch that is going to choose the winner. We have both got the same idea it seems. I am concentrating, but so is Chu Chu. It's like a chess game. Then I see how Chu Chu is dropping his left arm to his waist now and then. Normally he could get away with dropping his hand – he was such a fast boxer. But not tonight. I see my chance. He is looking to throw a light left from his waist. I slide to his left – Bang – I catch him a lovely punch on the chin. A hard right. Before he can do anything about it, he is on his arse. His jab is still on the way out, but stopped midway. His eyes are moving about and coming to rest – moving about and coming to rest. His fists fall on the canvas and his head's stretched up to me. He looks like he is searching for lost money and he is about to ask me if I have seen it anywhere. He is trying to come to terms with being on the deck and unable to get up. He was probably lining me up for that killer punch when I caught him. You can see that his mind's trying to get up but his body won't respond. He eventually staggers to his feet. The referee looks at him for a couple of seconds, puts his arms around him and declares me the winner. When a fighter's as far gone as that and the referee throws his arms round about him – it's like a mother with a baby. The boxer is helpless and the mother comes to the rescue and holds on to them in their despair. Even in a boxing fight there are beautiful things to see – if you look closely. We're all human beings doing the best we can with the talents God gave us.

Next stop – the doctors. I check it's not the same guy as the last time. But it is the same eye and that worries me a bit. I get eight stitches but I don't feel a thing. It's amazing how winning kills the pain. Best painkiller in the world – the glory of winning. As usual I can't wait to get home to my family and a wee bit of rest and some golf.

On returning from New York I have a pile of letters. Great. A cup of tea and my feet up as I plough through them. One is an offer from Maple Leaf Gardens in Toronto: a re-match with Frankie Otero from Miami. I phone the Maple Leaf Gardens to talk to the promoter and I agree to the terms.

Last time I fought Frankie it was Miami and it was roasting inside and outside the boxing arena. This time Toronto was just like Edinburgh. Freezing, wet and windy. Rain. More rain. And some more rain. I come in at three pounds heavier than when I fought him first time. I was very strong and I know from the first minute of the first round that this fight won't be going on for too long. I was out-punching Frankie right away and I was still out-punching him all the way to the sixth. He has been throwing fewer and fewer punches as the rounds go on.

By now Frankie has absorbed a lot of punishment. I have hurt him to the body and caught him a lot on the head. Two minutes into the sixth I catch him with a cracking right hand to the chin. Down he drops – clawing away at the canvas to get up. But there was no way he was getting up from that. Sometimes you wonder if your opponent is going to recover from a knock-down. But there are other times when as soon as you have landed the blow and he buckles – there is no way he is getting back up from it. The referee steps in and the fight is over.

After the fight while we were sitting talking in the hall Otero's wife came running in. She came right up and gave me a roasting for beating her man. Frankie followed her and dragged her off.

He was a nice guy and apologised to us for her outburst, but I could understand her feelings. My granny used to go to all my amateur fights. Man, she'd go crazy when anything went against me. She was not slow in letting her feelings be known to the public at large – to the crowd and the sometimes terrified referees. Good on you, Granny.

No sooner was I back home than I received an offer from Mogens Palle – a promoter who runs big shows in Copenhagen. He wants to know if I will fight Miguel Araujo, the current Italian champion. The fight is to be in Copenhagen's boxing venue K.B. Halle. Too right I will. A trip to Copenhagen would be just the thing for me. I am hardly out of training and I am straight back into it again. This time my focus is in a ring in Scandinavia – a bit different to imagine than the Gardens or Miami. But I bet it is going to be cold.

Before I went to Copenhagen I went to my doctor to ask him if he could give me something to boost my energy during fights – as long as it was legal 'cause boxers get carefully examined after each fight. He gave me a prescription to take to the chemist.

We arrived in Copenhagen in the morning and after dropping my bag off at the hotel we went directly to the weigh-in. I was introduced to Mogens Palle, the promoter, who was a fairly happy-go-lucky character, and I met a few of the other boxers – they were mostly Danish, Italian or French so there was not much conversation. When I met Miguel and shook his hand I instantly felt that there was a weakness in his armour, which can sometimes happen when meeting an opponent. I felt like I had already won the first round.

When I arrive at the stadium that night the second fight is just starting and I have some time to relax and prepare myself. Any boxer will tell you that on fight night he wants no interruptions at all. I decide to take one of the energy tablets my doctor prescribed. I didn't tell anyone about these, not even my dad – after all it was only glucose and I didn't want to worry him.

Anyway – my dad is getting my gloves ready and I am due in the ring in five minutes. I don't feel any more energetic than usual so when I go to the loo I take a couple more. Just then a steward comes in to tell me that the previous fight has been stopped so they're putting on a six-rounder before my fight.

Now, that's something I really hate – I'm ready to go, only to be told I'll have to wait half an hour or more. After sitting there for twenty minutes I start to feel a movement in my body like it's wanting to get on with the job at hand. I realise it must be the tablets starting to work. Then I'm up – shadow-boxing and punching the walls. Dad knows something is up. I don't remember much after this so Dad had to fill me on some of it later.

As we approach the ring I start up the aisles, shaking people's hands and kissing all the women. The crowd is going crazy. Here was this Scotsman in full tartan gear, about to enter the ring for an important fight, and all he wants to do is thank the crowd for coming!

My dad and Peter lead me to the ring and I jump right in there and start shadow-boxing. When I'm called to the centre of the ring I put my gloves strongly down on Araujo's and he looks startled.

Ding ding! First round. Out I come and throw a fast right hand that just nicks Araujo's chin. He falls on to the canvas, but gets back up fast. I can see he's absolutely shitting himself so I close in on him by the ropes and let go six combinations that hit the spot. Down he goes. The referee points to the neutral corner. I run to the corner and jump up on to the top of the pole. The Danish crowd are going crazy, shouting: 'Buchanan!! Buchanan!!' I join in – waving my hands in the air. The next thing I know Araujo is being led out of the ring and I am declared the winner. To this day I don't know whether it was because he just refused to go on or whether he was disqualified for not continuing.

Back at the hotel I confessed to my dad about the tablets. He wasn't too happy and I got a bit of a fright when he told me how I'd behaved.

Before I left Copenhagen I agreed to box there on the next two shows. But I was still hoping to get a call from Teddy Brenner or that there would be a contract there when I got home. But when I returned, although there was the usual pile of letters, none of them had an American stamp. Nor were there any phone calls either. It looked like Duran still would not get back in the ring with me.

My next opponent in Copenhagen, José Peterson, was a tough light welterweight from Puerto Rico and a very skilful boxer. I decided before I went in with him that I wasn't going to take any chances. And that was good for the fans because it turned out to be a great boxing match. Both of us relied on all our skill and experience to pull us through. I won the ten-round fight on points. But it was a hard fight mentally and physically. At the end I remember telling my dad I was glad it was over. So was he. After those relatively easy fights this one had reminded me how much boxing can take out of you. There was no way I felt like jumping on the corner post after this one. No way! I hoped my next opponent would not be so cagey.

I took Carol and three-year-old Mark up to Aviemore for a couple of days' break. Aviemore is great, up in the mountains in the Highlands. It's got the lot, but it is especially famous for skiing. And skiing is why we were there. If I learned anything up there it was this: just because you have a finely tuned body for one sport doesn't mean to say you will be good at another. In fact, it doesn't mean to say that you will be any good *at all* at the other sport. We went skiing on the slopes the day after we arrived.

To tell the truth, most of the time it was my arse that did the skiing. I couldn't stand up for more than a couple of seconds. Believe you me – when somebody tells you skiing is easy he is either a good skier or a good liar. I just couldn't get the hang of it. At one point I was going downhill and gathering speed. I tried that snowplough thing where you turn your toes in and make like a big chicken – but instead of making me stop it made me go faster – and faster – and faster – next thing I fell. And as I went down the handle of the stick hit me on the head. It was harder than any punch I have ever had in the ring.

I am getting a special set of skis made for myself. I'll wear one on each foot and have another – a giant ski – fitted to my ass. I had an instructor most of the time we were there. Give the man his due – he helped me as much as he could. It was like trying to teach a kangaroo how to box. But at the end of the day it was up to me to stay on my feet as long as possible. Just like boxing – only nothing like it. This crazy picture came into my head – me and Duran in the ring, boxing – only both of us are wearing skis. Can you imagine it? Trying to move round a ring with those things on. Maybe they should start that – comedy boxing. I'll not be doing it anyway. After a couple of days, the instructor gave up. I had been one of his worse students. He said that if I had been on my arse as many times in the ring as I had on the snow slopes I'd have never made it as a boxer.

I had another fight coming up in Copenhagen. So right after the break it's back on the roads at six in the morning. Although I must say that my bum was a bit bruised for a week after the skiing. I have got to keep myself in shape. I am into the gym in the evenings. I remember I was quite enjoying my training at this time. I had just got into my routine and I felt that wee break had been just what I needed.

The day before the fight I flew over to Copenhagen and checked into my hotel, only a couple of miles from the arena.

On the day of the fight I went to the weigh-in and met my opponent for the first time. Joe Tetteh from Africa. I knew his reputation. He was a hard man and not too many people in Europe would fight him. But Joe was growing close to retirement. It is one of the sad things about boxing – fighters continuing way past their sell-by date. And it's not just the money that makes them do it. I have heard that students in universities once they finish their studies keep going back to the buildings. They can't shake it off. They sit there sipping coffee, looking at all the strange faces. And that is just after four years. Imagine what it must be like to give up boxing after, say, twenty years? I just hoped that I wouldn't end up doing that. I sometimes had nightmares about it. I am in the ring and trying to throw the combinations but when I do they won't come out. And when I land a punch it is soft and ineffective. Terrifying – boxing with all that skill and experience in your head but you just can't get your body to perform.

I am not saying that is what Joe was like. He wasn't. He was still in great condition. But if the truth be told, Joe was over the crest of his hill. I go into the fight giving away about six pounds but I know I have the speed and punch to cope with that. I get a great reception due to my antics the last time I was there, when I'd jumped up on the corner post. But this is a much more sombre affair. I suppose that's because of the respect I've got for Joe. For the first couple of rounds I work fast at jabbing then moving – jabbing then moving. Looking for openings all the time. Sitting in my corner at the end of the second round my dad says, 'Ken, he is open to a right hand.'

I kept what my dad had said in mind when I was coming out for the third. I throw some good strong jabs then a right hand to Joe's stomach. I got the punch through quite easily and I heard him groan. It surprised me because no matter how over-the-hill a boxer is, it's usually well into the fight when you start putting blows through as easy as this. I thought to myself that now was the time to try a hard right. I test the ground with a couple of jabs and Bang! My right hits Joe on the chin. Joe's legs give way and down he goes. This time his eyes look clear but he still can't get up. The fight is over. Once again the audience started clapping and chanting my name, but I didn't feel as good as I had the last time I fought here. It might have been something to do with the fact that Joe was fighting well out of his league. That and the fact that he had been a hard, hard boxer in his day. Sometimes when you see a funeral going past it reminds you that one day you will be in that box. And nothing you can ever do in life can stop that. But in boxing when you see a man fighting past his prime you get the same feeling – but the thing is, it's not inevitable that you will end up like that. This is a train and you can get off at any stop that you like. But watching Joe on the floor gave me the shivers. I had a bad feeling in the pit of my stomach. I couldn't get into the spirit of the cheering.

I went over to Joe's corner to make sure he was all right. He was. I didn't go over there for praise but the crowd clapped – it was as if they were appreciating what I was going through. Who knows, maybe they were? Still, when I'd shaken off the doom and gloom at the end of that fight, there was no getting away from it: Copenhagen was a great place. I'd be back here by hook or by crook. I thanked the people and prepared to go back home again. Everything should have been rosy, but an image of Joe looking up at me from the deck kept appearing in my head like some kind of crazy ghost.

I have only just returned home, when I get a phone call from the secretary of the British Boxing Board of Control. And they don't phone up for an idle chat. He tells me I am wanted in Italy to fight Antonio Puddu for the European lightweight title. Certainly. I am the man for that.

I contact the Italian promoter who offers me good money. I am quite surprised at how easy it is. I don't even need to haggle. He wants me to fight Puddu in Cagliari on 1 May. I have agreed to a fight that gives me about three weeks to prepare. Usually you would give yourself three months at least to prepare for a European title fight. But I had been fighting and, apart from the José Peterson fight, none of them had really taken anything out of me. They were more like sparring bouts. So, all in all, I was feeling pretty fit – and pretty confident.

I didn't abuse my body. I am not really a cookies, buns and rock cakes sort of guy. So I brought up a couple of sparring partners from England, guys who came recommended. Not like the two in America who were going to go on strike if I didn't stop hitting them so hard. That's like a bricklayer going on strike because he has been ordered to work with bricks. I worked out harder than usual with these two excellent sparring partners. And they weren't averse to a hard punch nor were they shy of throwing a few hard punches themselves. We must have turned the heat up as high as it can go in sparring without it turning into an actual boxing match. It's a line and it is measured by attitude not amount and power of punches. There's an attitude for fighting and an attitude for sparring. Sometimes fights can be like a training session – but you still feel it's a fight. Sometimes a sparring session can seem like a fight – but you still know it's a sparring session.

But one thing is for sure: with training sessions like that under your belt your confidence just grows and grows. Men like that are as important to a fighter as his corner men – but they hardly ever get the thanks they deserve. Well – thanks, lads. One of those sparring partners was Ricky Porter. He was a welterweight – a stone heavier than me. And he had a reputation for being a hard hitter. I can vouch for that! So I had to move swiftly so as not to be on the end of any more of his punches than was absolutely necessary.

I found out that Antonio Puddu came from Cagliari and so he would be the favourite with the crowd. But things like that had never bothered me in the past. It is only a couple of times that I have fought in Scotland with the crowd behind me. Even the British title fight with Jim Watt doesn't count because half the crowd was behind Jim and half of them were behind me.

Out to Italy we went, and it's a great place to look at: rocky mountains and wee olive groves everywhere. We went over to the arena to check it out. As you can imagine, going to box in Italy and take home their title wasn't going to be easy. Especially as Puddu wasn't exactly a pushover. Some four years before I had gone to Spain and lost in a very controversial decision to Miguel Velazquez. Well – I wasn't about to let that happen again. At the weigh-in I looked upon Puddu as the challenger, and the underdog. I was the champion. This little trick can boost a boxer's morale. And it certainly did for me. The weigh-in went smoothly and off I went for some grub and some rest. Some hours later in the football stadium the bell went for the first round.

When I got into the ring the crowd seemed more interested than hostile. They never booed and that is what they usually do when the man from somewhere else gets in the ring. The Man From Somewhere Else – I like that. Maybe if they had given me a name – like 'Hands of Stone' Duran – they could have called me Ken 'The Man From Somewhere Else' Buchanan!

When I am in the ring I don't bother with what is going on outside it. It didn't affect me when Puddu got the biggest cheer from the crowd, rightly so because he was the local hero. I knew I had to keep on top of him every second of the fight. Pressure him like I did Laguna. I had to make sure that the judges knew I had won every round. It's always very difficult to get a points decision in these kind of places. But for all my confidence I had to make sure I didn't get caught with any of his wild swings.

The first round we're really testing each other out, trying to see what the other man can do. The second round both of us are going forward now and then to take the fight to the opponent – just to see how they react. After the second round I say to my dad that this is not going to go too far because when we are inside he doesn't like mixing it with me. He gets out of any close work as soon as he can. I go out for the third to box and probe, testing him out. I am gaining in confidence as the fight goes on.

I don't think I lost a round. Puddu was tiring, he was throwing fewer and fewer punches, and was taking more and more of mine. There came a point when almost every jab I threw was catching him. Even the fans were not shouting too much.

They had gone quiet. And that in itself is an eerie thing. Not that I was actively listening – but when the constant buzz and roar of a partisan crowd dies away you notice something missing in the atmosphere.

By the time the fifth round bell rang I had the full measure of Puddu. I knew his weaknesses and I pursued them relentlessly over the three minutes. In the sixth round it was all over. I threw some jabs and a couple of body shots. I backed off and Puddu came at me – I caught him with a jab followed by a cracking right-hander and he hit the canvas like a bag of tatties. Or *patata* as they call them in Italy. He went down like a sack of *patata* – that sounds a lot better.

I waited for the booing and baying of the crowd, but it never happened. To my surprise the crowd were clapping like hell for the performance I had put on. Now that was really surprising. They appreciated a good boxer in Italy, it seemed. I was the new European champion. Unexpectedly, the crowd went mad with delight for me as the referee held my hand up in the air. I suppose they felt that they had just watched a first-rate fight. And even though their countryman was beaten, it was by a better boxer.

With the European belt now round my waist, I felt like a million dollars. I was on my way back up – the only thing left now was the return with 'Hands of Stone' Duran. Hide and go-seek Duran he should be called.

When I won the fight, I was mobbed in the ring. The crowd even took me out the ring and held me up in the air, like I was their champion. Ken Buchano. I was carried shoulder-high by those Italian boxing fans. They carried me through the ground and right in to my dressing-room.

Later that night I took my dad and my corner man, Freddie Hill, out to a restaurant. One of those authentic Italian places. It was like being in the movies. We walked into the restaurant chatting away, minding our own business. As far as I was concerned we were four strangers out for a meal. Then I noticed everybody looking at us. At first, I thought it was because they had clocked on that we were strangers. But that's not what it was. They stood up, first one, then two, then three or four here and there. Soon the whole restaurant was standing. I was just wondering what was going on when they all started clapping. I realised what it was all about. They clapped us through as we were shown to our table. The whole country had probably been watching the fight that night on the telly. So this event was like Scotland being in the World Cup final (dream on!). We were treated like royalty the rest of the night. There was complimentary wine and liqueurs from the owner. Waiters were there every time we so much as looked as if we needed anything. It was one of the best meals I have ever had. And the company – it was all fantastic. We all had a great night. We left Italy thinking it was a wonderful place. Equal in my book to Copenhagen. We were all dying to go back to Italy as soon as we could. Who knows, Puddu might ask for a return.

Back in Edinburgh I was warmly welcomed by the press and the people. Here I was with the European title, and yes – it was good to get the attention. It's amazing what winning does for you. I'd be special for the time being. Everybody gets their fifteen minutes' fame. Well, by that accounting, I had had much more than my fair share of fame so why bother about past resentments? I realise that not everybody can be a winner but it gives you a nice glow inside.

I took my usual rest and then got back into some light training again. I knew it wouldn't be long until somebody somewhere would want to challenge for the European title. Sure enough, I got a phone call. My first defence of that European title was to be against Leonard Tavarez of France. Once again, no British promoter was prepared to put up a reasonable purse for me to defend my title in Scotland or in England. I couldn't understand why, for there was money out there for the making as the foreign promoters showed, yet they wouldn't go near it. So once again it was out with the suitcases.

To be honest – I had travelled around the world so much that I never really had a chance to unpack my suitcase. I could pack it blindfold. I never knew where I'd be off to next. Forget Man

From Somewhere Else. They should have called me Man in a Suitcase. Paris was my destination this time. The city of romance. Most people had labels of countries and cities on their suitcases. Well, I was a different kind of tourist. When I looked at my old brown suitcase every dent or scratch was a boxer's name. Duran – Tavarez – Laguna – Navarro – you name it!

I had in fact boxed Tavarez twice before in London, beating him on points both times in 1968 and 1970. But I didn't let that slow me down in my training, or dampen my conviction. As any boxer will tell you, having beaten a fighter before might be good for your confidence, but it means nothing on the day of the fight. On the day of the fight it is you and him in the ring and what is at stake is your reputation. The facts were – Tavarez was a good boxer and a hard target to hit. And he can only have improved since the last time I met him. I had to pay him the utmost respect or I might be letting myself in for a shock. Keeping your mental guard up is as important as keeping the gloves up in the fight.

I went over to Paris the day before the fight – we flew over. (I had again trained hard at the Sparta Club. I loved my old amateur club in McDonald Road – it's a private club now. What an atmosphere!)

Edinburgh to Paris took only a couple of hours. You were hardly up in the air than you were back down again. This time there was nobody trying to wind the windows down. You might think it's a bad idea to arrive in the city so close to the fight – but I was in really good condition so arriving the evening before the fight would do me no harm.

Sitting in the dressing-room waiting to be called is always tense. Always quiet. My dad said, 'Look son, you've beat Tavarez twice before in London.' I remember him holding my gloved hands in his as he spoke. 'But keep this in your head. You might have come on a lot since then, but don't forget – so has he.'

My dad was thinking the same thing I had been thinking on

the way over. That is how close we were tuned in when it came to the boxing. I answered him with only a nod – your concentration is so high-pitched just before a fight it's like you're on drugs. That is probably why I remember the tense times the clearest. My dad went on. 'Don't be taking any chances out there tonight. Keep away from him. Jab and move. I want you to use that jab to build up the points – when you see the opportunity drop in that right hand we've been practising.'

I am still nodding away to his every point. Anyone watching would think I wasn't listening. But I was – intently. I could picture me in the ring – Tavarez coming at me. Me tilting to the side to slip his jab and bang – dropping the right in on his chin. I could see Tavarez falling and me winning the fight. My dad was talking as I imagined all this. 'Remember – keep cool, calm and collected – if you lose the head, you lose the fight.'

OK, Dad. I won't let you down. I won't lose the head.

Out we went an' I am repeating in my head, *Lose the head, you lose the fight. Lose the head, lose the fight . . .*

And I didn't let him down. I have always listened to my dad. Especially in matters of boxing. And I can tell you this: Tavarez had improved – and so had I – it was a good job too. It turned out to be one bloody fight. A great contest. There are some contests you want to forget. Others you can't really remember. There are fights you remember for the things that went wrong. But there are fights you remember because as boxing matches they were excellent. This was one of them. Tavarez was on top form, and he was going for it in a big way. Coming at me all the time. Then he'd break and I'd go for him. The crowd were on their feet from the very start.

Early in the bout both of us were cut above and under our left eyes. That old left eye again – giving me trouble just when I don't need it. Both our noses had gone and our lips looked like we had been smacked in the face with a cricket bat. Three good smacks each – at least. Today, with the rules a shade stricter, I think several of my fights would have been stopped.

All I knew at this point is that I was in the ring with Tavarez – the new improved model. And I was finding it pretty hard. As the fight progressed I started getting some good shots through to his body. Thank God for that because I thought I was never going to influence any change in the fight. It seemed he had peaked and was now on his way downhill. The training and the underwater swimming were paying off again. From then on in, with each blow Tavarez lost interest. I could see my opportunity was about to come. He had put his all into the fight. But I must say – his all was not enough. He was starting to slow and when your opponent does that it is only a matter of time before you catch him.

In the fourteenth round I hit him with the best punches of the night and he collapsed to the canvas. He struggled to get up – his neck craning up and his eyes looking around. Half of me wanted him to get back up. Not so that I could pound the punches into him but so that the two of us could be standing at the end of the fight. It was such a ferocious battle we both deserved to be there at the end with our dignity intact. I felt that I was ahead on points anyway. But he never got back up. The referee saw he was in too much trouble and called a halt to the fight. That's a laugh when you think about it. Both of us had had faces like a butcher's floor since early on. If Tavarez could have at least stood up and held on I think the referee would have let him. Hell, in those days, some referees would have let you pull knives on each other and not stop the fight. But he wasn't getting up. He was trying but his body wasn't responding – like that dream or nightmare I keep having. Tavarez was beat. I was still European champion. It felt great even though the cuts on my eyes were hurting like hell.

Like in our earlier two bouts in London, Tavarez was superb in defeat. He put his arms around me and thanked me for the title fight. He said, 'You're the best, Ken.' There is something about that sort of hard contest that brings two boxers together. At that point Tavarez and me – we were closer than brothers. It would bring a tear to a glass eye.

When I had any bad cuts after a fight my dad always made sure I was treated right away. One look at the cuts on my eyes and he was into action. He had a taxi waiting outside the arena to take me to a French hospital. It was all a blur winding through the streets of Paris. It isn't like Glasgow or Edinburgh, where the streets are usually deserted at night except for people out for a night on the town, people actually live in the houses right in the city centre of Paris. So there are hundreds of people about – it is a city full of life. It would be a great place to live – buzzing. They should do that in our cities: move the people back into all the empty buildings in the central areas. Then there wouldn't be so many people on the homeless lists in Edinburgh and Glasgow.

So we're tearing through the streets of Paris. And I mean tearing – have you ever seen the French drive? Fuck me! Now I know where Tavarez gets his bottle from. He probably realised earlier in life that it's much safer in a boxing ring than it is trying to cross a French road. There we are laughing away in the after-fight euphoria – blood trickling down my face and the taxi driver's trying to talk about the fight in French. It was crazy – like a scene from Monty Python. I must say that I was well looked after in the hospital. Treated like a king I was. Nine stitches over the cuts. Even the prick of the needle going in and out and the eyes swelling up didn't feel too bad – as I've said, winning the fight is the best painkiller ever. I wish I could bottle that and sell it. I'd be a millionaire.

showing guts

However, when I got home it was time for some serious thought. By now, as far as boxing was concerned, I'd had a good kick at the ball. I'd be thirty in a few months, and I could retire if I wanted. My record only showed two losses in fifty-eight fights – one in Spain and one in New York. My pride would be intact and I had a few bob put by. I was seriously thinking about retiring. I didn't want to end up like one of them guys I was telling you about earlier. The man in the nightmare. Joe Tetteh from Africa on the floor looking up. A man boxing far past his prime, boxing on name rather than ability. Also my daughter, Karen, was born a couple of weeks before the Tavarez fight. With Carol, Mark and Karen all needing a dad, and my business interests growing, did it still make sense to risk serious injury after I'd achieved all I'd ever wanted.

I think I would have given it up at that time, but there was one thing niggling at me, all the time nipping away in the back of my head: Duran. I still wanted my return with Duran. They were calling him the hardest man to beat in the world. His career was rocketing – with a few hand-picked opponents – fair play to him, he was knocking them all out. But where was my return? I had gone the distance and the fight had been stopped in a controversial manner. I knew I could beat him if somebody would only give me the chance, but, alas, it did not happen. My phone calls to his people were ignored, and the call that I was waiting for never came. There was more than just the personal thing keeping me and Duran apart. Money and politics are what count in boxing. Duran was going to make a lot of people a lot of money in the coming years. He already had made a lot of people a lot of money. There was no way they were going to take the risk of me taking his title away. There is more money in an unbeaten champion than an old champion coming back. That is just the way it is in boxing. I started to realise that I'd never get a return with Duran.

I am shouting to get a shot at Duran but then the British Boxing Board of Control in London nominate me to fight Guts Ishimatsu, the WBC world champion. They have contacted his manager and he has accepted the bout, but it was to be in Tokyo. I was a bit annoyed they hadn't checked with me first. I mean, I am the other half of this equation.

It was a great opportunity for me as Guts Ishimatsu had been beaten by Ismael Laguna before I beat Laguna twice. Don't get me wrong – I never went to Tokyo thinking all I had to do was turn up and the fight was mine. No boxer in their right mind would think like that. But, by the form book, that is exactly what should have happened. But the Japanese boxing fraternity didn't want that title leaving their islands, and so they weren't going to make things any easier for me.

Before I left for Japan, I had trained as hard as ever. I knew this would be my last chance for a world title so I brought over a sparring partner, Alphonse Viruet, from New York. I had used him on several occasions while in the Big Apple. He was good and he had a very similar style to Guts. We sparred many rounds in my Edinburgh gym over the next two weeks.

On the way over to Japan I was thinking that there would be some unusual customs to observe at the ringside. I guess I'd watched too many films about samurai and geisha. It was probably no different from their image of Scotland – that we all run about in kilts, eat haggis and play bagpipes. When I arrived in Tokyo I was surprised and happy to see it was much the same format as in all big fights anywhere else in the world. You have reporters running about asking questions – half of them you can't understand. They are speaking English, it's just that you haven't got used to the accents yet. Half of my answers they can't understand because I am Scottish. They were all asking each other what language I was speaking. God knows what they wrote in the papers. I couldn't read them anyway. You know the reputation the Japanese have with their cameras – well, imagine an event where there is actually something to take pictures of!

There were photographers wanting every angle of your face to see if they could trace any scars which could be highlighted in the story. Flash flash flash. My eyes were sore with it all the first day.

But it's a great country. We stayed in a lovely hotel on one of the main streets. I done my roadwork at five in the morning so as to miss the smog and the hordes of people going to their work. If you think London has got a lot of people, wait till you see this place. It was very strange going through those streets. In the early morning light, with the streets all but deserted and most of the signs in Japanese, I felt like I was on another planet, never mind in a foreign country.

Whenever I left Edinburgh for a fight, I was always in top condition. So the ten days that I was in Tokyo prior to the fight all I did was tick over. Sparring and running, sleeping and eating. I had done all the hard work – now all I had to do was keep my speed and stamina at that level.

For six days I am picked up by a chauffeur at my hotel and taken to the gym the promoter has assigned for me. And what a gym that was. They had laid on the best gear and the conditions were superb. The Japanese have got a reputation for taking existing things and improving them. Well, they do the same with boxing equipment.

Four days before the fight I have been getting good write-ups from the Japanese press. They have come along and watched me sparring with the partners supplied by the promoters. They are so impressed they are actually writing Guts Ishimatsu off, but that happens a lot before a title fight. The papers were concentrating on the facts, that although Guts is the champion he had been well beaten by Laguna. A man I had beaten twice. So therefore . . . But like I have said, that hardly counts for anything on the night of the fight. Reporters at the gym where I was working out were writing I was the better of the two men.

However, for the last night of my sparring me, my dad and my second were taken to a different gym. I should have clocked on that there was something going on, especially with the fast moves that had been pulled on me already in the boxing game over the years. But as I have said, I was always an easy target when I was concentrating on the fight and my fitness.

On our way through the streets of Tokyo in the car, we were told the gym we had been training in was closed down for essential repairs. We never thought much about it at the time. I mean – the days I had been in the place it was in perfect condition – whatever the repairs were they were not showing up as faults in the building at all. But I had not a pang of suspicion, even though you should always be wary at this stage of the build-up.

On arriving at this other gym I simply got stripped off for my last four rounds of sparring. I entered the ring rolling my shoulders about and not thinking of much except the impending spar. Then I noticed something was different. I peered at the guy across the other end of the ring. My sparring partner had put on a good few pounds and a pair of platform shoes – he had suddenly grown six inches. I asked what had happened to my other sparring partner. They said he had hurt himself at work. I asked if it was serious and was told yes it was.

I asked what he did, thinking he might work on a building site or a steelworks or a shipyard where getting hurt, or even killed, is something that can happen any day. There was a pause. They were all giving each other funny looks. I soon found out why when one of them told me that he was a window dresser.

Well! Me and my dad and the second fell about the place laughing. We couldn't get up. I was doubled over like something out of a cartoon. Like the wee robots on the Smash advert. I'd been in the ring for a week sparring with a window dresser – that is one I wasn't telling the lads back home. No, sir! Funny thing was, the more we laughed, the more the Japanese laughed back. And I think they knew that we were off our guard. And we *were* off our guard, which is why what happened that day happened so easy. There was nothing we could do to see it coming.

But I still had to know what happened to my window-dressing sparring partner. And when we found out that just made us laugh all the more. They told me he fell off a ladder while dressing a window and sprained his ankle. Once we calmed down a bit from that they gave us some more – it was better than Billy Connolly. The window where my sparring partner fell was a display of women's underwear. Kinky knickers and bras! So we laughed and they laughed back even louder.

Once we stopped laughing it was time to get on with the sparring. I'll tell you this, it was a right good warm-up – laughing. They should put a stand-up comic in every gym. In all the laughter we had almost forgot what we were here for. Once I started sparring, it became clear what was really going on. The window dresser and them laughing louder than us were distractions. They were at it.

My new sparring partner wasn't exactly trying to knock me out, but he was up to something. There's that certain look in their eyes and movement in their bodies when you know they are doing more than sparring. In the third round this guy threw a left – as I was slipping it over my shoulder he rolled his thumb into my eye socket. Ya bastard! It was really sore. There was nothing I could do. Before you could say Muhammad Ali my left eye was giving me a lot of pain. I went right for him. I punched him four or five times and he dropped to his knees. I jumped out of the ring and back to the dressing-room. My eye was so swollen my dad decided to get me to a hospital there and then.

At the hospital we discovered air had blown my eye up. The doctor put some padding on the lump and bandaged my face tightly so that the pressure on the lump would push the air out from under my eye. Now I couldn't do any sort of light training at all, only a bit of walking. I also had to hide from the press. If the papers had printed a photo of me all bandaged up, it would have killed the gate. Nobody is going to turn up to see a fighter with a big bandage on his head. I had to be as discreet as possible. I used the waiters' lift and staircase to get in and out of the hotel. Thinking back now, it's a wonder I wasn't spotted since practically everybody else in the country was Japanese. And none of them was wearing a turban!

My dad asked for the fight to be put back a week – no chance. If I did not go ahead with the fight I might never get another chance. I had to make a decision, and I had to make it now. My eye won't stand up to too many punches. Remember this is my vulnerable left eye. With a big lump on it – it might open up like a kipper the first blow Guts lands on it. That is when I began to think the ten-foot-high sparring partner had done it deliberately, aiming for the left eye. If that was it, he had done a good job and earned his pay. As ever, you could never know who it is that's put him up to it. Your first thought is that it's Guts' camp, but it might as well be a gambling syndicate that has a lot of money riding on Guts. Or even the opposite – because of the favourable press reports, the public might be putting everything and the kitchen sink on me to win. With all that in mind you can see that these people will go to any lengths to save their money. But one thing is certain – no matter who is behind all this, Guts will already know about my eye even if the press don't. He will be going for it from the first bell. That's what they will have told him to do. They might even just be telling him that I hurt my eye in training. But there will only be one thing in his mind: his title. So as I said – I've got a decision to make. I ask myself, do I go out there hammer and tongs to knock Guts out early or do I box him and hope I don't take too many punches? Since it's what I do best, I decide to box – hoping the eye holds out.

It is no fun going into a fight already sporting an injury. But I think I boxed well. My confidence was rising as the fight went on. I was doing well till the eighth round. I had scored points, kept Guts' blows at bay and was well ahead. Then he came at me. A barrage of punches were thrown at my head. I covered up well but some got through and closed my eye. Things were difficult from then on in. I was holding my own. But because of the restricted vision I was getting caught with some stupid punches I just didn't see coming. Rights coming in on my blind side.

The bell for the end of the fifteenth round rings. I feel within myself I have done enough to win, but I have heard that saying many's a time. The decision went against me that night in Tokyo. Well – I guess that is what life is all about.

That defeat by Guts made me all the more determined to continue with my career. It was something like the Duran defeat in that I felt in both of those fights I had been cheated and that dirty tricks had been pulled, though Guts had done nothing wrong. I have always prided myself in being a gentleman. But unfortunately not all those involved in boxing are like that – both inside the ring and out.

I got home on a bit of a downer. But I soon shook that off with some time with my family and generally hanging about. In the meantime I had agreed to defend my European title against Giancarlo Usai of Italy at the same football stadium in Cagliari where I had beaten Antonio Puddu earlier last year. We were really looking forward to going back. And we were especially looking forward to going into that restaurant again. Yes, Sardinia was the place for me. By Christ – never before has a place turned out to be so different when I visited it again.

I agreed terms with the promoter and the fight was set for 25 July 1975, a month after my thirtieth birthday. It's funny the wee decisions we make. I take a fight – not giving it much thought: just another fight and on with my life, on with my quest to regain the world title. I mean the defeat in Japan was disappointing, but it didn't dent my confidence – I knew I could have won if I hadn't gone in with an injury. So going to Italy was to keep myself in there, focused on boxing. Little did I know that this fight was going to make me retire from boxing.

the italian job

Here I was back in Italy at the same venue, with the same promoter, staying in the same hotel, looking forward to going out for a meal in that same restaurant. All that was different was the fighter.

I saw Usai for the first time at the weigh-in. He was as tall as myself and looked as though he was a bit useful – very fit-looking. Everything went well at the weigh-in, but going into the ring I felt a sense of foreboding. It wasn't right. It wasn't the same as last time, when I was clapped out of the ring and carried high. When I jumped in the ring I could sense hostility. I had become a barometer to the atmosphere and it was bending the needle hard against danger. My sense was to be proved right.

For eight rounds I punched Usai's head off. I began to wonder why he took the fight if he wasn't even going to try. He could at least go for it in flurries, try to knock me out. But nothing. It was like a training fight only all that hostility meant that my adrenaline was flowing all the time. Usai was making no impact whatsoever on the fight – apart from the fact he turned up. During the ninth round the referee pushed his hands between our heads to break us up and accidentally stuck his finger in my left eye. You might be thinking aye – right – that referee done that deliberately but I don't think he did. You can usually tell these things. I took it as an accident. I said nothing to my corner but on coming back after the eleventh round my dad spotted there was something wrong. I was starting to take punches in the fight that I had avoided easily earlier on. I told my dad I was seeing three of Usai.

He asked which one I was throwing punches at. I replied that I was going for the first one, as he was nearest, but I kept on missing him, and he was catching me with counter-punches. Dad explained that I must have double (or treble!) vision, and that I should go for the second one. Then, if that doesn't work, I'll know it's the third guy.

So out I went for the twelfth round, seeing three referees and three Usais. The crowd are screaming holy murder as I begin with some light jabs at the second Usai. But he's not there, and as I'm bringing back my arm to my chest I get a belter from Usai's right hand. I know it's the third Usai I have to aim for – if it's not him them I'm out of there. Yes, I've touched him with my slow wandering left jab: he's number three. And now that I know which one is real I have to go for him. Not only because I can see him now but because there is no point in me trying to counter punch because it looks to me like I am fighting an octopus. I flick out the left hand and connect with Usai. I can feel the strength of my jab shoot his head back and I now know I am back in business. I could sense his disappointment that I was finding my range again, I struck home with jab after jab. Looking to drop in the right hand wherever I could. I never let him off the hook. I went for him, closing him down no matter where he went in that ring. He must have thought a new man had stepped into the ring with him. Did he really think I was that bad a boxer? There was a real look of surprise on Usai's faces as I came back into the fight with a bang. I started catching Usai (the one at the back) with the best shots I had thrown all night. I was scoring points like a man possessed. The crowd didn't like it. Not one bit. I can understand it. First they thought their man was taking a beating, then he comes right into the fight and it looks like he is going to win. Then he is taking a bigger beating than the one at the beginning of the fight. Usai was starting to wilt. He had obviously thought my missing with so many punches was down to me being tired. I felt fresh and fit enough for another twelve rounds.

I feel really good and I continue to jab Usai's head off in the twelfth. I think he is ready to get to know my right hand. There is only about a minute to go so I let fly a right hand after feinting with a light left jab and bang it lands right on his chin and he collapses in a bundle at the side of the ropes. Usai looks up while his right hand grapples with the ropes. He had the look he should have had as the referee began his count. The look of a man who one minute was certain he was coasting to a victory and the next he is on the deck wondering where it all went wrong. As I looked on him after the referee signalled the fight was over, I wasn't ready for what happened next. It seemed the crowd all came up with this almighty roar all at the same time.

All hell broke loose in that stadium. I couldn't believe it was the same place where they had carried me aloft after the Puddu fight. It is a funny game, boxing – a funny game indeed. But this time the joke would be in trying to get out of that ring alive. Some joke. Paper cups, cans, programmes and bottles came flying into the ring. There was a tremendous bang as one of the big ring lights above was shattered. The glass showered down on my back cutting me everywhere. Meanwhile, Usai was still lying on the canvas waiting for the stretcher to arrive. As I was kneeling in my corner my dad rushed over and was trying to cover me. Next thing, a bottle hit him on the head, splitting it open; blood was pouring out on to his white shirt. It was at that moment I wondered how he felt all the times I had been burst open in the ring, because looking at my dad with the blood running down his face was one of the worst moments of my life. He was very groggy and looked like a drunken man. Our main object now was to get across that football field and into the dressing-room.

On the way, I was throwing punches at any Italian fans that get in the way. Even after twelve rounds I still had a little bit left in me. It was at that moment that I heard a voice call out: 'It's OK Kenny, we're the British Army. Keep running and we'll make a passage for you to get back to the dressing-room.' It was marvellous of these guys not only to have been there, but to give us all a free passage back over the football ground. I'll never say our troops can't fight – they took on the whole stadium that night. Thanks lads, the British Army did us proud.

The police told us to wait in the dressing-room till all the fans had gone and they would give us an escort back to our hotel. Meanwhile, my dad was taken off to the hospital to get six stitches in his head. I remember lying down flat on the table and letting my corner men pick out bits of glass from my back. I can assure you it was very painful. All the time what was going through my head was, *Is this all worth it?* My dad was in hospital and I had a back full of shattered glass. After all the glass was out I was able to get into the shower and give myself a good wash down. My back was nipping when the soap got into the cuts. As I was dressing I remembered I had left my European belt in the ring. When the bedlam started and my dad had got hit I forgot all about it. I told the police and they went out to the park to have a look for it, but it had disappeared. I wasn't surprised. With the way this night had gone there was no way that belt was going to be lying there. From being one of the best places we had ever visited, Italy – in one crazy hour – had turned into one of the worst places we had ever been to.

Back in the hotel we were all a bit subdued, to say the least. We settled down and were watching the news on the television. We can't understand a word, but it is all there in the pictures. There are the scenes from the fight and the bit where my dad gets hit on the back of the head with the bottle, but he didn't go down. And on the telly you could see the bottle came across that ring with some force. I wished I could get my hands on the bastard that threw it. But to me it was a great feat that my dad managed to hold on to the ropes and not go down when he was hit. Maybe his genes gave me the power to stay standing when I needed to.

The following day the Italian papers are full of the riot started by the Italian thugs. Usai is still in the hospital in an oxygen tent from the beating I gave him. Through my interpreter I asked him to convey my sincere apologies and wished him a speedy recovery. After a week in hospital, he was soon boxing again. And us? We are desperate to get on a plane back home. I am afraid the visit to what was once our favourite restaurant would have to be postponed – indefinitely.

Before I left Cagliari I asked about my European belt and trophy. They said it was stolen when the riot broke out. I knew that, but what were they going to do about it? They said they would look into it and get in contact with me when they had any progress. I guess it adorns some Italian boxing fan's sideboard. Any chance of getting it back, mate? If it is not too much trouble?

Once back home with the European title but no championship belt or European trophy. I wasn't feeling too great about continuing boxing. I called my dad and told him I was going to write to the British Boxing Board of Control and retire. He didn't try to talk me out of it. He just told me to give it a couple of days and if I still felt the same to go ahead. He was right behind me. He always was, my dad. It broke my heart the thought of retiring. But it had to be done if not for emotional reasons, then certainly for medical reasons. My eye had taken some pounding over the years and now it was really bad. I was still seeing double from it. I would never have passed a medical with the problems I had. Everything was a bit uncomfortable for me now that I was seeing two of everything. My doctor fixed an appointment with an eye specialist. He diagnosed double vision and short-sightedness in the left eye – the eye that got cut most often. So what was to happen?

I was going to have to wear glasses for the rest of my life. The thought didn't exactly thrill me. But what could I do? I have tried contact lenses since, but I dropped them putting them in or taking them out, and I kept losing them. I hate all that fumbling about and trying to stick them to my eyeball. I don't want to go fifteen rounds with a pair of contact lenses every other day, so I gave up on the idea.

With my boxing career finished, I retired as the undefeated British and European champion – and my doctor telling me, 'Enough is enough Ken, spend *mair* time with your family and business and enjoy life.'

And he was right. Like a lot of top-class sportsmen I had neglected my wife and family, not deliberately. I had always done it with the idea that, even if I was spending very little time with them while I was training and fighting in foreign countries, the money I would earn would make us secure the rest of our lives. We would be able to spend more time together when I was at home and in my hotel, or going on holidays.

It was now time to try to rectify my life now that I was going from one extreme to another. I didn't have to get up at six in the morning and pound the streets anymore. Goodbye roadwork. Goodbye five miles in heavy boots, with weights in my hands. No more sweating my guts out in the gym with sparring partners four nights a week. From now on my life was going to be different. I decided on a change of career: my new restaurant was about to open at my hotel on Ferry Road.

For somebody who is more used to eating in restaurants than running them it was going to be fun and games. I had to be guided by the people I employed. I had to interview waiters, chefs, bar staff and decide on who was the best for the job. I knew all there was to know about the boxing game, but I was still a complete novice in the catering trade. After a wee while observing the comings and going of the place, I was not happy at the stocktaking figures as they were not as high as they should have been, so I started to investigate. Ken Buchanan – super sleuth. I kept tallies on kitchen chits and bar bills . . . discrepancies began to show.

I was always one for going the distance and after a few months it was time to dispense with someone. He would be going on a technical knockout. I informed him of his rights and sacked him. He denied everything, of course, and he wasn't a happy chappy. I'll not repeat what he called me because I don't speak his language. Just as well for him, probably.

Funny how things are when you're giving somebody the boot. It seemed all wrong for me; I felt like a cop arresting a criminal. But to be honest – I have always felt that people who steal from others in business are thieves and should be dealt with accordingly. That is what I kept telling myself. I had a tendency to feel sorry for them when they started the tears and the pleading. But this was business. I had to be hard. After he was shown the door, things went along OK. The new man appreciated the chance to take an opportunity in life.

The hotel was doing fine and I soon found that I had extra time on my hands. I joined Ratho Park golf club. I had enjoyed many games there with my friends, even though I was no great golfer. But now that I was spending more time doing it I realised just how much it relaxed me. It took my mind off the whole boxing thing. It was good not having to compete at such a high level. Not to compete at any level, in fact. The pressure was off and it was great. There were times when a six-foot putt on the last green meant you either halved the match or won it. If I missed it was going to cost me a pound, and everyone knows what that means to a Scotsman.

Between the work I put in at my hotel and helping at the gym, my time was mostly taken up. I was having a very enjoyable life. Hunky dory. I was able to relax at home in the evenings with Mark and Karen. Things were going well. Life was plodding on. Everything seemed fine – just fine.

But something was not right in my head. Niggling away there like somebody jabbing at you the whole fight. Not bothering me much at first but building up and up until it's just a bloody nuisance. I was beginning to have withdrawal symptoms from the boxing. I guess I was a boxaholic. And another thing – I was beginning to understand how it was that so many boxers carried on long after they should have retired. I didn't want to end up the man in my nightmares, but I had to involve myself in boxing somehow. I was addicted. I didn't want to fight – I was doing my best to avoid going down the has-been road. I thought about it and came up with a great solution: I took out a boxing manager's licence and got myself a couple of local fighters to manage. I still went into the ring to spar with them. My wife thought I must be mad having a bad eye and still sparring. But if you look after yourself you hardly ever get roughed up at the sparring, except in Japan. Looking back now, I guess my wife didn't understand what it's like to give up something you have dedicated your life to since the age of eight. To tell the truth – it was impossible. And it was going to prove to be much more impossible than even I had ever thought it would be.

comebacks

The years went by: the hotel and bars were doing well, and I spent a lot of time running them. But it was not easy going from world champion to hotelier. There were still the little scams to look out for, as when a waiter told me he was returning to his home country because his family wanted to go back. A few weeks late, I got a call from a local garage demanding payment for the repairs and service to the waiter's car, as he'd asked the garage to bill us. Why the garage owner didn't check with me first – he was a regular – I don't know. But my waiter had left a false forwarding address, so I had to pay up.

My career as a boxing manager had come to nothing. There was an aching chasm in my life. It seems boxing had been much more of my life than I had at first thought. And I suppose not being involved in the world I wanted to be involved in had taken its toll on my moods. With hindsight, I should have seen it coming but it was a shock when it did: Carol wanted a divorce.

About the middle of 1978 I had to sack two employees at the hotel and so told Carol that I wouldn't be able to go on holiday that year with her and the kids. So she went to Blackpool with Mark and Karen for a couple of weeks. Bad move, Ken. Bad move!

I often wonder if it's a good thing to sit down and look back where things went wrong in your life. On her return home, she wanted a divorce, saying I was concentrating too much on the hotel and not enough on her. At first I thought she was joking, but no. After a while, we put the house up for sale and I moved into the hotel. At least living there meant I was always available, if anyone was unable to turn up for the shift. I gave Carol all the proceeds from the sale of our house, plus more money, and all the furniture was transferred to her new house in Edinburgh.

What I did not at first realise was that on that holiday Carol had met Jeff, who was to be her future husband. So as not to make things difficult for the children, we agreed to divorce. However, when she moved down to Northampton it made it very difficult for me to see Mark and Karen, though we had agreed on my rights of access – and I loved taking them to the baths or the park and out for a meal.

Because of all the complications between English and Scottish law, I was advised that it was better for the children's sake not to try to pursue things through the courts to assert my rights. Then suddenly I got a demand from her lawyers that she wanted her forty-nine percent of K.B. Enterprises paid to her. I had been advised to make her a shareholder in the company, when I set up various accounts to handle the money from my boxing purses, as there had to be at least two shareholders. As it was this company that owned the hotel, the lawyers were demanding I paid her £49,000 as the hotel was valued at £100,000. I had been given to understand that she was a shareholder in name only.

Sadly, I did not have that sort of money to spare, so I was forced into selling my hotel because of the divorce and the way K.B.E. was set up. It has often been reported that I had to sell it because I was in danger of going bankrupt, or because I was a bad businessman. But nothing could be further from the truth. When I bought it, I paid £25,000 for a large house that was doing bed and breakfast. I turned it into a good hotel, that I sold for £100,000, so even though I had to give Carol nearly half of it, I still came away with a good profit after eight years.

Carol came out of our divorce well. Why did I let that happen? Mark and Karen were only nine and four years old respectively. I wanted this major upheaval in their lives to go as smoothly as these things can go. Iron out as many ruffles as I could. What was money over a man's love for his children? If you feel I was taken to the cleaners – I let myself be. For them.

Looking back now, I suppose the life I led was not so fulfilling for Carol. Maybe she saw the whole boxing and fame thing in a romantic light. Many women would have liked to have been in her shoes. But like every other walk of life the problems set in. And they did with us. It would be the same with a travelling salesman, who never sees his wife for months on end. And on top of that there was the press intrusion. More than anything, that can destroy a relationship. To be honest the press have hardly left me alone since my early days. They still portray me as a poverty-stricken, alcoholic ex-boxer. But from an ordinary working-class point of view, I would look like a guy who has a couple of bob in the bank and conducts himself in a reasonable manner – all things considered. They wouldn't see me as the down-and-out the papers try to make out that I am.

But back to Carol. OK, she had our lovely house and her own car. She never needed to worry about where the next meal's coming from. I gave her and our kids all the love a husband and father could. For, although I was away for long periods, when I was home I didn't have a nine-till-five job, so I spent a lot of time with them then. Time the ordinary Joe wouldn't be able to because he would be at work.

Carol had a lot of time on her hands when I was away. We had a talk and decided we should set up some kind of business with the money I was making. I set up Ken Buchanan Enterprises and bought a big house in Ferry Road, Edinburgh. After building work was completed, it became known as the Ken Buchanan Hotel. Carol's parents, Anne and Frank, moved into the hotel and ran it for me, while Carol started off helping them with the books, wages, VAT, tax, national insurance, and all the other admin tasks, though she gradually lost interest.

By Christmas 1978 I was not a happy man. My life felt empty and the year was fading away. I decided to have a good look at myself and decide if I could go back to the boxing. Could I make it in the ring after such a long lay-off? Could I avoid being a man fighting on his name and not his ability? I was spending a lot of time on my own with my own thoughts. And my head was filled with boxing when it wasn't filled with grief. Or more accurately – I filled my head with boxing to cope with the grief.

Eventually, I had to give in to the inevitable. I made a comeback in Denmark against Puerto Rican, Benny Benitez. It was my thirty-fourth birthday, 28 June 1979. You would think I would have learned sense by then. But, no, not me. Not the underwater swimmer. Not only was I making a comeback, but I didn't want to fight a patsy. Most fighters making a comeback work their way in gently. A couple of easy fights before you take on anybody hard. It gets you up the ratings a bit, too. But I wanted a good opponent. Benitez proved to be just that. He made me work hard, but no way was he going to beat me. I was in the ring with the demon of grief to help me along. And anybody who has been in that situation will know exactly what I am talking about. I won the eight-round fight on a unanimous decision. I must say it felt good to be back.

A couple of months later I was back fighting a tough little guy from Italy – Eloi de Souza. It was again over eight rounds and I ran out a clear winner. I was getting hungry for more fights. I was back in the ring again and raring to go. And – I was quite amazed at how fit I felt. Years before, I would have thought a thirty-four-year-old man was ancient and past it, but here I was fit and strong and winning fights.

Next thing Mogens Palle offered me a European title fight with Charlie Nash of Ireland on 6 December. It was a good offer – two comeback fights and I was lined up for a European title bout. Even though I had only been back fighting for a couple of months, I took the contest anyway. At my age you might not get another chance. The fight was to be over twelve rounds in Copenhagen. And I can tell you that was one hell of a fight. Charlie was a good southpaw and he had an impressive record. Indeed, I felt I had done enough to get the verdict. Charlie was a good sportsman. He said to me before the decision was announced that he thought I had won. 'I think you have got it, Ken,' he commented. Good on you, Charlie.

But the judges thought otherwise – I lost. And the loss cost me dearly. If I had won it, that would have put me in line for some big-money fights all over the world, and maybe another crack at a world title if things went well. I was devastated. Things were not looking so good.

Early in 1980, I got a call from a promoter in London who wanted me to fight Najib Daho. Well, we all know who he is now. Then he was an up-and-coming prospect that everybody was watching. The fight was to be over eight rounds in the Sporting Club in Mayfair. I agreed to the fight. Even though Daho was up-and-coming, I felt my experience would be too much for his youth. And I was right; I could tell by the third round that I was going to win this one.

I remember in the clinch in the sixth round telling him to take his time because he had hardly hit me. But no, you can't tell kids anything. Daho tried to keep on top of me, hoping he could catch me with a decent punch. He knew he was losing on points so he was trying to knock me out. Coming out for the seventh I felt that one decent right-hander would finish it. If I could feint a left jab then drop a right hand in on his chin. I was right again. If only these bairns would listen! I waited till he threw a couple of jabs. As he was about to throw a third, I threw a cracking right just over his left arm – his arm was coming from his waist – Bang! I hit the target and he was down and out. His jab was flapping out there in mid-air as he went down.

I was invited to fight in October in Birmingham against Des Gwilliam, a light welterweight. No lightweights about at the time wanted to fight me, so I guess my reputation was still worth something. Maybe I should have fought some patsies on the way up and made hard work of it so that I could get some bigger fights. But that's the way it goes.

The contest with Des Gwilliam was a good fight. My dad and I felt quite happy at the new weight, and I beat him on points. Believe you me I had to work bloody hard to keep out of his punching range. And you had to do that with Des because he could punch. Hard!

I was then matched with Steve Early to box an eliminator for the light-welterweight championship of Britain, as there weren't any lightweights around at the time. Here I was yet again looking at another title eliminator fight. I had by this time given up all thoughts of ever meeting Duran again. In the years I was out of the ring, Duran had catapulted himself to a fame that was untouchable. I, on the other hand, had the memory of a punch on the balls to haunt me for the rest of my life. My fight with Steve Early was to be on 26 January 1981.

Steve Early was a good big light welterweight and I allowed him to get too many shots at my body. I should not have done that. Over a fight body shots will eventually weaken you no matter who you are or how fit you are. I could feel the extra poundage he carried into the ring on the end of every punch. It was a bit too much, and my legs weren't as flexible as I wanted. Maybe they weren't as flexible as they once were and would never be again. I didn't get into a good enough swing for the fight, never got any rhythm going, because he wouldn't let me. In the end, Steve won the bout and went to box for the title.

After that, everything went downhill. Fast. Looking back – although I didn't admit it to myself at the time – I was too old. Age had caught up with the underwater swimmer at last. But the thing that drove all the other boxers who boxed well past their sell-by date was now driving me. I lost three fights in a row. I was becoming the man in my nightmares. I lost one fight to Langton

Tinago in Zimbabwe. I think I only took that fight for the trip to Africa. But it is hard to tell my true motivation because I never knew what it was myself at the time.

I got a call from Salisbury in newly independent Zimbabwe. They wanted to know if I would take a fight with Langton Tinago over ten rounds at nine stone eleven pounds? Why not? I mean, he is a good boxer but my experience has always helped me. I thought I could box him over ten rounds easily.

When Paddy Byrne, who accompanied me on this trip, and I reached Salisbury, I had a light work-out in the same gym as Tinago. As I was working out I felt there was something missing, not quite right. My jabs and crosses were a fraction out. Not so that anybody watching would notice. It's a gut feeling; an intuition. Everybody, no matter what profession, has had that feeling. Your shit just isn't coming together and you can't fathom out why. By the time the fight came up I realised I was in for a hard time. And to make matters worse, all the judges and the referee came from Salisbury. I would have to knock him out not once but two or three times to win. Ah, well, I accepted the fight.

And to cap all that, it turns out that Tinago was an excellent boxer. But even though I was feeling a bit out of sorts I still had enough of the old magic to out-point Tinago. I also landed a few good cracks on him. By the end of the fight he was hanging on to me for fear of falling. This is how I found it hard to believe it when he was awarded the decision two to one. Looking back the two to one decision proves my point. They were all partisan judges – for even one of them to give it to me on points was something.

But this wasn't the place to start arguing with the officials. We kept our mouths shut in case I didn't get paid. But when we got the money and packed our stuff we made our way to the airport right away. I wanted out of this country and quick. It was one of those places you felt you could disappear and nobody is going to come looking for you. And if they did – nobody is going to admit to ever having saw you.

Boy, was I happy boarding the plane back to London with a wad of British cash in my wallet. It is a strange way to be earning money. I was nearly thirty-six years of age. I guess I should have been stopped from taking any more unnecessary punishment, especially since the doctor had told me years ago never to box again on account of my left eye. I knew my career was at an end, but there was nothing I could do. Something inside me was driving me on. If I was a runner, that would have been OK. I could run marathons and go in for age-group championships. But I was a boxer and all that matters in boxing is what you can do in the ring. It is a ruthless game. And it must be said that I actually enjoyed the training and everything about it. It gave me a buzz. I couldn't give it up. I was like a drug addict. I know I should have stopped – but I had been boxing since 1953. It was heavily in my blood.

There was this young, useful boxer called Lance Williams knocking on the door and I was asked if I could fight him at Wembley, 24 November over eight rounds. I accepted the fight. This was like an exhibition rather than a bruising battle. There were no big punches thrown throughout the fight. Lance was a nice boxer who moved too well for my liking. The wee bugger could have stood toe to toe with me. But no! He was going to jab enough to get the points verdict. I have to admire him for the way he was able to hit me without getting tagged himself. He was boxing in a style similar to the way I used to box. Ach – it was time to hang up the gloves.

Well, that was that. Christmas and New Year were over and I had just started a new job. I was back working as a joiner. To be honest I felt as much comfort with a nail-bag round my waist as I did a Lonsdale Belt. There was no pressure except to tap those panel pins home and not leave any half-crown marks on the wood. I could handle that sort of pressure, no problem. A good joiner can lose himself in his work. And I think I got lost a few times.

One time I was working in a block of offices in Glasgow – renovations. I was sitting down having my lunch with some of my workmates. My workmates only knew me as Ken. They never knew I was Ken Buchanan the boxer because I had a three-day beard, glasses and a cap. A couple of guys in suits from another part of the building came up and asked me for my autograph. When they left one of the workers said, 'Jesus, Ken – you must be some fuckin' joiner!'

I continued to go along to the gym three nights a week. I'd spar with some of the amateurs who were waiting for a boxing show to come up. I just couldn't leave boxing alone. So when Les Roberts gave me a call asking if I would fight at the National Sporting Club against George Feeney at nine stone eleven pounds a few days later on 25 January 1982, I took it. Les explains that George is not a big puncher, and that it should be a nice work-out for me. Shite, Les! George was undefeated and was waiting for his turn to fight for the British title. Come that October, George stopped Ray Cattouse in four rounds to win the title. George then went on to defend a couple of times to give himself a Lonsdale outright. Oh, aye, Les – he's not a big puncher. Right!

Les and me went back a long way. He was the man who got me my first pro fight back in '65 – in the exact same place he was asking me to fight in now. I told Les I hadn't been in the gym this year at all. If he was going to be such a blatant liar, then I was joining in too. So he begged me to take the fight. The show had hit a few snags. I could save his skin here. I said OK, but don't tell anybody I have not been training. I told him that knowing fine well he'd tell George's manager that I had not been in training. Actually, as always, I had kept myself quite fit.

There was great excitement at the National Sporting Club that night. Entering the hall they gave me a tremendous reception. After all I had been the world champion. I can still hear the applause today. When the bell goes for the first round George is out like a shot to get on with the job. Obviously, Les had told him that I had not been training. Also, as he was about to fight for the British title he wanted to look good. He wanted the powers-that-be to see what he could do. He did that by winning the fight, and he had won fair and square. I wished him all the best in his forthcoming title. I know I have said it before, but this time I really meant it. Right there in that ring. Fighting boxers I would have beaten easily in my day – I decided to give it up. Really. No bullshit. This was the end.

It was an emotional scene. I took the microphone from the MC and thanked George for the fight. I thanked Les Roberts for asking me back to have my last fight in the same hall and same ring I'd had my first pro fight in back in September 1965. I announced my retirement. I did have some tears in my eyes but what the hell – I had been a boxer since 1953. All I ever wanted to do was be the best in the world. Like some of the other people in my class at school who went on to become lawyers or doctors. All I ever won at school was scraps and the bible prize. I did what I wanted to do. To this day I am the only boxer ever to win a world boxing title as a professional from Edinburgh.

I left the ring in tears as the members started singing, 'For he's a jolly good fellow!'

I went back to being a joiner. It's what I know other than boxing. Although a few people might argue over that. The years rolled by. One night I came home and got a call offering me a fight against Johnny Clayton, but it was not licensed by the BBBC.

I could be doing with the quick money so I said OK and the following night I went straight round to the Sparta. It's funny how you give something up, but when you go back to it, you feel you have never been away. You automatically slip into gear and drive off. At first it feels like I have never stopped, but the first couple of days on the roads kills you. Running ain't what it used to be. I am puffing and panting like an old man.

The first week is the hardest: running up the hill that is two miles into my run. I could see it far enough – and I remember the old Ken – the Ken that used to spring up there like there was no incline at all, take the hill and want to go back and do it again. I used to treat running down any hills as not running at all – now I am glad of them – they are like a rest. After a few days of killing myself I wanted to phone Joe and say I have changed my mind, but the embarrassment would be too much for me. I had to face the fact that I was getting older. If my head wasn't, my legs were.

In the gym I sparred with all the guys available. Boy, did they put me through it. My body was telling my brain, but my brain wasn't listening. The strange thing is, years before, when I was probably training twice as hard, it felt twice as easy. Now that I am only training half as hard as I did back then, it feels twice as hard on my body.

There were no problems at the weigh-in. Fight time! I enter the ring to the sound of 'Scotland the Brave' over the tannoy. God knows what Johnny came into the ring playing – there is too much noise. Away we went at it – hammer and tongs.

I won the fight by a knockout in the seventh round, but it doesn't matter who won that fight really. It was my last. My dad and I went home on a bus from London to Edinburgh. That was a long, lonely journey. I thought about my whole boxing career as we whizzed through the night. I had been there and touched levels that very few men ever see. I was happy with what I had done with my life. I went home, I picked up my tools and went back to the joinering.

Within the week I got another call, asking me to fight Jimmy Revie, who was a cracking southpaw who had done very well as a pro, winning the British featherweight title. Again I won in the seventh round, but that was definitely it. I retired from the ring after that fight, and haven't boxed since. But I still could not get Duran out of my head.

when scotland went to harlem

I got a chance to go on the Panamanian version of *This Is Your Life* in 1994. They wanted me to meet Roberto Duran. I said I wouldn't mind coming across if he agreed to fight me again. It was a joke – they're hardly going to set up a ring in a telly studio and have us two fighting. But if they had said yes, I would have fought him. But either way, I did say I would go over and meet Duran. The press back here, as usual, made something out of it, making me out a raving loony of an ex-boxer still looking for that one fight to boost me back to stardom. So in the end I didn't go.

If they set up a fight between me and Duran even now – I'd take it. I think they could sell it for millions round the world. And I bet two old codgers like us could still whip up a bit of a storm in that ring. If there's any promoters out there that want to arrange it – give me a phone. Mind you, I doubt if Roberto could make 135 pounds.

But clearly it sparked something in me, and it came out the next year. I was still working as a joiner, on the tools, for builder Alan Lamont. But there was something building up inside me. It had been growing since 1972 since that punch on the balls in Madison Square Garden: Duran. He had become my biggest demon, and I had to get rid of him. Exorcise him somehow or Duran would haunt me till my dying day.

I had watched him continue his career as mine slipped away. Whatever he achieved, I still felt he didn't deserve to be world champion, rolling in the dough and the glory.

I keep seeing a big picture in my head of June 1972 and Duran is jumping about the ring with my title. I go white-hot with anger every time I think about it. And nothing can cool me down. All I ever wanted was a return fight, but Duran stayed well out my road. Every time I was in a position to ask for a fight – there was some excuse. And you can't really blame his people for keeping us apart. So here I am working as a joiner more than twenty years later and my head just can't take any more. Any time I have tried to talk to another person about it they say, 'Ken, it's just one of those things.'

But it's not just one of those things, because if it was it wouldn't be bothering me. For the rest of the world it might be just one of those things, but for me it is *the* thing. And by now I am old enough and ugly enough to know that it has to be dealt with. And those years have not been easy. If I had a pound for every time I have been asked if I would have beat Duran in a return fight I would be a millionaire. And every time I got asked that question my heart broke just a little bit further.

So – I am tapping panel pins into a sheet of plywood in August 1995 and it comes to me: a blinding flash. I couldn't stop myself if I had wanted to. I went to Alan Lamont's office and packed in my job there and then. He was surprised. He thought I was happy there; I was. But he seemed to understand how I felt when I told him what I was going to do. To give him his due, he tried to talk me out of it – but there was no talking to me. My mind was set. He told me just to leave my tools there and he would look after them until I was ready to come back. I was off to New York to confront Duran face to face. We were going to find out who was the best man for once and for all.

I flew from Edinburgh to London. They must have thought I was a bomber or something with the tension of my face. There was only one thing on my mind: Duran. I got a flight to Kennedy airport. Here I was, anonymous, on a plane going to America and to be honest it felt like it was just the day before I was fighting Duran. It was that fresh in my mind's eye.

We landed in America and my heart was pounding. I thought Teddy Brenner from Madison Square Garden would be there with a contract for me to fight Duran. Now *there* would be a venue for a fight. I caught a bus from the airport to the terminal in the city. I noticed adverts for bed and breakfasts all over the place so I wrote down a couple of numbers. I phoned some but they had trouble understanding my accent, so the next one I called I put on a phoney American accent. I asked if I could have a room for a couple of weeks and she said, 'Sure, no problems, what time'll ya be over?'

'I am just hopping in a taxi now so I'll be there in half an hour.'

I caught one of those big yellow taxis and told the driver where I wanted to go. He had already started to drive but he put the brakes on and turned to me in the back. He was white. 'Hey man, do you know where that address is?'

'Of course I know – I gave it to you.'

'But man – you're white.'

'And?'

'You're a white guy, man!'

'I know that – I am not daft.'

'But this is an address in Harlem!'

'So what! I have already told the lady I'll take the room.'

So he shrugs his shoulders and says something I can't make out. But it's probably not complimentary. Off we go through the streets of New York. And I am looking about. Trying to spot any of the places I had been to before – maybe Madison Square Garden – but the streets seemed different. Even the people looked different. New York wasn't what it used to be. As we whizzed through the streets the driver never said another thing. I kept looking out and thinking what was I doing? One man in a city of ten million people, trying to find another single human being among those ten million people.

For a minute I felt like a lunatic. But what had to be done had to be done.

We arrived in the street in Harlem where the bed and breakfast was. I gave the driver his fare and a tip and he is offski – nearly before I can shut the door. I caught a few people looking at me. But that didn't bother me. Nothing much frightens me at all now. I climbed the twelve steps to the front door and rang the bell. I could feel eyes drilling into the back of my head from everywhere. Nothing happened. I tried the bell again with my ear pressed to the door. I could hear voices and music but there was no ringing. I banged on the door a couple of times and soon I could hear somebody coming. The door opened and this woman pokes her head out. She is about five feet nothing in her socks. Her name is Lucy.

'Yes?' she says.

'I phoned you from the terminal!' She stares at me like I am an alien. 'You said you had a room – for a couple of weeks.'

She stares at me – stares at my case – her mouth falls open.

'But man – you is white!'

'Jesus – you're the second person today to tell me that!'

'You're white!'

'Yes, brilliant! Christ, I know that!'

I smile, she smiles, and lets me in.

She shows me to my room, muttering all this stuff about a white man in Harlem and laughing to herself. But to me she is just like any wee woman you might meet on an Edinburgh street. She asks me if I have eaten yet.

'Naw.'

'Pardon me – have you eaten yet?'

'No.'

So when I've got my stuff sorted out in my room she takes me in her car further into Harlem. It was already dark. She takes me to Mrs Wells' restaurant. Up the stairs we go and some people are looking at me. She opens the door and goes in. I am right behind her. The place falls silent. Nothing. Not a fork or a knife scraping on a plate. Mouths are hanging open. There is a white man in the doorway. That is what they all seem to be thinking. Wow! There are about twelve black guys and two black women drinking at the bar and they have all nudged each other and turned to face me. But I didn't give a shit – to be honest there are times in your life when nothing matters – and I think people pick that up. I went straight to the bar and ordered a bottle of Bud. Lucy introduced me to Mrs Wells as Mr Buchanan from Scotland and the tension went down in the place. Mrs Wells, a happy, attractive woman, asked me what I wanted to eat. The menu was right in front of me.

'Steak, medium, baked potato and a side salad.'

'No problem – coming right up.'

I take a slug of the Bud and turn in my chair. The man at the end of the bar says, 'Hey man, are you Scattish!'

'Yeah – I am Scattish,' I says back.

He has got a bashed nose like mine and you can tell he has done a bit of boxing in his time. He turns and talks to his buddies. I know they are talking about me and Scatland and all that, but I try to be as cool as I can. He is throwing a few jabs and punches like he is explaining a fight or something. And it's a ring fight he is explaining not a street fight. I was simply drinking my beer and keeping myself to myself. I was still waiting on my dinner arriving when the same guy shouts up the bar again.

'Hey, man, do you know Ken Buchanan?'

I nearly choked on my beer. 'Yeah – I know him – the boxer!'

I don't let on, just to see what they say about me – but it's all good stuff. After fifteen minutes chatting away, Mrs Wells come out with my dinner. By this time the gang know my name is Ken, but they don't make the connection between me and Ken Buchanan.

Mrs Wells asks if I want my dinner at the bar or at a table. I decide to stay at the bar and start tucking in. A few minutes later she comes back and asks, 'Is the food all right, Mr Buchanan?'

'Aye – it's great.'

Well, it takes a couple of seconds, but the guys register the Ken – the Buchanan. Then there is an uproar. One of them stands up and shouts, 'Hey – you is Ken Buchanan – the guy who fought Roberto Duran and got hit in the balls!'

'Yeah, yeah, that is me but that wee shit would never give me a return. I mean – I have often wondered why they gave him the name – Hands of Stone!'

Well, that was that. I settled down into the bar and a night of drinks and chat. We all started telling boxing stories. Some of the guys had actually been at the Duran fight all them years ago. It brought a tear to my eye that they remembered me. It made the whole Duran thing seem much easier in my head. The fact that there were guys in Harlem who knew who Ken Buchanan was and that he had been done out of his title. It turned out to be a great night. I had them all in the palm of my hand with the stories from the boxing game. None of them would let me put my hand in my pocket unless it was to draw out my hanky.

They in turn told me a million stories about Harlem – man – that is one hell of a place. As the night was drawing to a close, I asked the barmaid if she could call me a cab, but the two big guys at the end of the bar said, 'Forget it – we'll take the champ home.'

And they did. When we all parted I said I'd be back in a couple of days' time – once I'd found Duran. I did go back to that place a few times and there were more and more guys turned up to meet me. At times I felt like Jesus with his assembled flock.

After about ten days looking for Duran in all the gyms and bars, I decided I was never going to find him. I mean if he was in Harlem then he'd have known somebody was there looking for him five minutes after I arrived. So, after two weeks in Harlem, I went back to Scotland. Scatland. When I got home, I went down to Alan Lamont's and asked for my job back. 'No problem,' he says. 'How did you get on?'

'Och, OK I suppose – aye – OK.'

I set about getting my tools which were still on the floor in his office where I left them, and made my way up to the building-site. At least I had plenty of stories to keep the lads going – and I did – right through the rest of that job – it was Harlem this and Harlem that – you would think I had been there for years.

Life for me had always been go, go, go, so to be back at my old trade wasn't as much of a let-down as you might think. There is something good about being in the one place – having an easy routine – not having to pound the roads at six in the morning. I had some strange dreams for weeks after I came home. Me and Duran battling it out on the streets of Harlem. For try as I might, I still couldn't, and can't, put Duran to sleep. I don't think I'll ever get rid of that, as I am constantly reminded about him by boxing fans wherever I go. Who knows – maybe one day I'll meet him and we'll talk it over and he'll admit that he got the title by a dirty punch and a bad decision. That might get him out of my head. It just might. But all the same it won't stop me from wondering what would have happened if we had never met.

Soon after that the joinery dried up for a bit and I was looking for work. Miller Wilson, a former boxer from Cumbernauld, offered me a job at a company that was looking to recruit people immediately. What they used to do was paint the outside of buildings, big fancy houses, factories and all that. I explained I was not a painter and that I was not interested in doing all that, but he said all I had to do was go along in the van and give the guys a hand. I said that was all right, and things were looking good. I was getting paid for it so I wasn't bothering. I'd put a good day's work in no matter what I was doing. That lasted a good bit of the summer. Then I was advised to get out of the company at once, because it was in danger of going under. It wasn't the money he was on about, he also knew the way the press was with me in Scotland, and that they might give it a story like BUCHANAN IN COMPANY BANKRUPTCY, or some other headline like that. They already had me down as a business failure with my hotel – which

I wasn't – but I took his advice and left.

I wasn't keeping too well at the time either; I couldn't sleep at night. So I went to the doctor and I was prescribed sleeping tablets. I don't know what it was he gave me but they certainly knocked me right out. Nobody had been able to do that all my years in the ring.

It was my mate Ricky's birthday on 2 December and he'd come home drunk from the pub. I took him up the stairs and pulled his trousers off over his shoes and flung him into bed. I was taking it easy because of the pills. The effort of lifting Ricky up the stairs and into bed must've done something, because leaving his room I started to feel really tired. Really sleepy.

I went to my bed in the middle room on the first floor. Ricky was in the other one, and this guy Murdo was in a third room. We'd always had this feeling that there was something not right about him, and I never quite trusted him. Ricky was the same so we always kept one eye on Murdo. He was one for the watching, as we say in Scotland. One for the watching.

So I'm lying out for the count in my bed. My girlfriend, Ann Marie, had stayed in the house with me the night before and I got this feeling there was somebody in the bed with me. Because of the sleeping tablets I thought it was Ann Marie but something was telling me something was not right. Not right at all. While trying to wake up I feel this hand down my pants. I tried to waken up but the pills were strong. I wasn't responding. I was like a boxer on the canvas willing to get back up but can't. I summoned up all my reserves of strength. I had to wake myself up. I struck my head on the wall a couple of times and that woke me. I says, 'Who's that?'

'Murdo,' he says.

This rage sweeps through my body. A rage like I've never felt before. Ever. Even over Duran. A car or something went by and I caught a glimpse of him bollock naked in the bed. And he was smiling, a half-baked sheepish smile.

I just fuckin' banged him one, right on the face. He fell out the bed, whimpering. Squeaking like some kind of injured animal, but he wasn't injured enough. I had to get my hands on him. He started crawling towards the door. I could only see him the slither of light that came in under the door. And the shadow of his body. He opened the door and got out. I was bouncing all over the place with these pills. Trying to get to the door. My head was clearing but very slowly. My legs were like rubber, as the sleeping tablets are fully effective and I've been in bed for several hours. I just see Murdo going into his room and closing the door. But my mind's clearing and my legs are getting better with every step I take. I could hear him cowering in his room. I got out into the hall and by now my head had cleared enough to realise roughly what was happening. And the more I realised the angrier I became.

I kicked that door open and ran in. Now I could see the bastard: sitting on his bed whimpering. But there was plenty of light in his room. I laid into him. The first punch caught him and he went reeling back to the window. The next hook skited off his face and I hit the corner of the window ledge with my knuckles. Blood was coming out. I broke a few bones in my hand. I laid another few into him. To tell the truth, and I know it sounds vicious, but I couldn't hit him hard enough with the thought of him in my bed. Each punch made me madder and want to hit him with a harder blow. I don't know how many connected with him and how many with the wall. During the whole thing I was bouncing all over the place. One heavy hook missed altogether and I fell against the bed. I hit a big metal thing coming up at the top of the bed. They weren't big beautiful beds, but this thing hit me in the back – on the seventh vertebrae and knocked a wedge out of it that will never go back again. I also broke my little finger and three of my own ribs giving him a doing.

Ricky came running into the room and pulled me off, but I still wanted more. I went down the stairs. The rage was still in me. I got a fuckin' knife and was about to go back up. Ricky came down the stairs. He told me he wouldn't let me go up the stairs. I'd have to go through him.

'Let me by, Ricky.'

'Kenny, you'll have to kill me before I let you ruin your fuckin' life over that! Now give me the blade.'

Eventually I gave Ricky the knife. He was a good mate, and he saved me from getting into deep shit that night for at that moment killing him was the only solution I could see. Perhaps I was lucky because I can look after myself. If I hadn't been, he could possible have done what he wanted and there was nothing I could have done about it. In some ways I was glad it was me – what if he'd chosen someone young or defenceless instead?

Ricky and I left the house, with Murdo lying upstairs. Ricky phoned a pal and told him what happened. So they called an ambulance took Murdo to the hospital, where he was stitched up and spent a couple of weeks. That's the last I seen of him.

I reported Murdo to the police and they went to the hospital and charged him. The next thing I heard was that he went to Falkirk to stay and six or seven months later he was given a heavy doing there, too.

The day after the fight. I went to my doctor and told him what had happened and how I'd picked up all these injuries, for I was hurting all over. I was sent to Monklands hospital where they x-rayed my hand and chest. When I told the nurse where I was in pain, particularly around the ribcage, she also x-rayed my back. I was on painkillers for almost a year afterwards. I also reported the incident to the criminal injuries, but as we all know such bodies take ages to reach a decision, and at the time I didn't know just how badly my back was damaged.

But fortunately, there was soon to be some good news: the year 2000 was to be a great one for me.

into the hall of fame

I thought, apart from a few guys in Harlem, I had been all but forgotten by the boxing fraternity in America, but that was not the case. On Sunday 26 December 1999, I found out that I was to be inducted into the International Boxing Hall of Fame. Man, was it uplifting news. That washed away all the bad things. To know I would be alongside such great fighters as Marvin Hagler, Sugar Ray Leonard, Floyd Patterson, Joe Frazier, Willie Pep and Muhammad Ali.

I have to say that I burst into tears when I heard about it. Even afterwards, I am still not sure it's true. After all the bad things it's hard for a good thing to sink in. Now, after thirty years, I was to be recognised. I was stunned by the honour. It was a handy way to finish this book about my boxing days – as if God sent me a happy ending. I am the only living British fighter to receive this honour, while the only other Scottish boxer to be honoured is Benny Lynch, the flyweight champion who died in 1946 aged just thirty-three.

But there's a big difference between the Hall of Fame and the everyday life of an ex-boxer. Here's a funny example. My good pal Rab Bannan has been running the Barn boxing club in Coatbridge for about a million years. Coatbridge was the first town in Scotland to get a licence from the British Boxing Board of Control to run a boxing show. He's got a great wee club and I'm behind him a hundred per cent. He invited me to a boxing show to celebrate the millennium on 27 April 2000, in the Kirkshaws club, where there'd be tickets at the door. So my dad and I went. The bouts were good and we had a great night. At the end I was invited in the ring, and gave a wee speech. They presented me with a lovely silver salver.

When I got home that night, I was making a cup of tea, and my dad asks for a wee look at the salver again. His face was puzzled as he read what was engraved on it.

'C'mere son,' he says. 'Eh – is there not something wrong here?'

'What,' I says, 'What's wrong with that? It's a good wee salver.'

So my dad reads it out: 'To Ken Buchanan, *1997*.' The two of us fell about laughing. I phoned and got a hold of Rab.

'What the fuck's this?'

'What's what?'

'It's the year 2000 and you hit me with a salver dated '97.'

'Aye – that's right Ken – you never turned up for that show in '97 – so I kept it for you.'

Both of us fell about the place laughing.

That was to be my last award before going to America for the Hall of Fame. Before I went to America I decided one thing: there was no way I was going to make an arse of myself this time. I was not going to give the press the satisfaction of ridiculing me again by saying I was drinking and all this nonsense. So I stoppped drinking on 28 May 2000. I've not drunk since and I don't intend to; I feel a much better person without it. One day at a time.

The last time I fought officially was in '82 or at the dead end of my career, but it was even longer since I won a major title. It was way back in 1975, twenty-five years ago. And, as that time passed, my career lost its glitter and died out. Once I accepted it was all over, it was much easier. Now out of the blue – this. Right back into that intoxicating world of cameras and attention. To be recognised for a career I gave the best years of my life to. Over the years the significance of my achievements has diminished in me. Now – it's all back into perspective. I can see that what I done was unique. Without being egotistical – I can see how they want to list me up there as one of boxing's all-time greats. And writing this book too has helped me realise that I deserve it. All I ever wanted was to be the best in the world. Now I'm going to be remembered forever for it. That is a fantastic feeling.

I got a card from a few of my mates before I left for America. I liked what it says on the front:

Those who achieve success
Are those who take a dream
And make it come true.

It moved me.

So I had a big going-away night with the boys in the domino team at Moriarty's pub in Cumbernauld. They gave me a great send-off. Back into the world of boxing after I had thought I was just another forgotten casualty. I must say, when I went to bed that night, I found it hard to sleep.

I get up at eight o'clock, nervous but excited. I'm off to America. I shower and shave. I still can't believe I'm off to be inducted into the Boxing Hall of Fame. Formally set up in 1989, the International Boxing Hall of Fame is based in Canastota, New York State, and honours those fighters who have made a major contribution to the sport. Each year a four-day event is held in June to welcome the latest additions. This time, I was a part of it.

I don't know how many times I check my suitcase. And every time I check it, all the things I need are still there. Nothing missing. I'm pacing the floor like an expectant father. Listening for the toot of the taxi. The taxi was ordered and paid for by Donald McLeod, photographer for the *Scotsman*. And with my track record with newspapers I'm starting to think it's not coming. Even though I like and trust the reporter that is going with me, there will always be that nagging suspicion.

But the taxi arrives at the door and off we go. When my dad

and I arrive at Glasgow airport we are met by a horde of photographers and reporters. They all want my last words before we fly off to the International Boxing Hall of Fame.

They've changed their tune. And talking about tunes – two pals of mine from the Black Watch are there to pipe me off. I answer the reporters' questions and pose for photographs.

The atmosphere in the airport was great. People from all over the world watching this man in the Buchanan kilt getting his photo taken. Most of the Scottish people know who I am but there are some curious looks from the foreigners. They probably think I'm a Scottish singer or something. I have always felt comfortable in a kilt and I have always made sure that people did not miss the tartan. I have always been proud of the clan Buchanan.

The take-off is amazing. It's like old times again, me and my dad in a plane being treated like VIPs. And my son Mark and wife Lauren are to meet me over there. Great. Life couldn't be better.

We met Mark and Lauren and one or two Scots lads in Newark and flew up to Syracuse. It's about 300 miles from New York; Mark filmed the whole thing on video. When we arrived at Syracuse airport there was a couple of guys in their kilts with a piper playing 'Flower of Scotland' as I got off. A rush of emotion caught me unaware and it was a second or two before I could compose myself. My whole being was lifted to a level I used to experienc at the height of my boxing career. It was great to be Scottish; it was great to be in America. From that moment till Monday 12 June my feet never touched the ground. Floating like a butterfly – not a sting in sight. A luxury limousine met us and drove us to the hotel. Very nice.

The organisation for the inauguration was perfect. I never for one moment worried about where I was to be at, say, ten the next morning or seven the next night. Everything was taken care of. Every detail. The male and female security staff were always there to guide me to my next meeting.

You might be under the misapprehension that Canastota is a big, flashy American town. So was I when I first heard of it. But it's not. Here I was in a village of about 1,500 people. Canastota doesn't even have taxis. You can walk everywhere – even if you're ninety. But in the world of boxing, Canastota is as big as New York. Everybody in the place know each other by their first names. But there was a few other names there. And the villagers called them by their first names, too. In the four days I was there I bumped into world champions like Marvin Hagler, Ken Norton, Ernie Shavers, Carlos Ortiz, Carmen Basilio, Alexis Arguello, José Torres, Juan Laporte, 'Bone Crusher' Smith, Aaron Pryor, Ruben Olivares, Gene Fulmer, Kid Gavilan, Joe Frazier, Matthew Saad Muhammad and Howard Davis to name just a few. It was like a school reunion, only everybody in the class had become world champion boxers or contenders.

There's always a lot of talk about ex-boxers being punch drunk and in ill health. I suppose what happened to Ali helps to fuel this myth. But it has to be said that each and every one of the fighters who attended this induction was in great health and good spirits. Some of them even looked better than they had when they were fighting. When you're at the peak of fitness your cheeks hollow out and to an untrained eye you can look sick. Like you've been on a crash diet.

I didn't meet Duran. But there was no way he was going to be there. It turns out that he had a fight within the week. When you think about it it's amazing Duran is still fighting. He ended up winning an NBO middleweight title, yet he's only seven years younger than me and I was nearly fifty-five. But good luck to Duran. He's a fighter. If he wants to fight let him get on with it.

In Canastota I must have signed about five million autographs, and spoken to hundreds of people. At various times of the day I had to be at a specific place but that ran like clockwork. I'd sit down and answer questions from the press, or from the public. What are you doing now? What do I think of certain boxers? Who was the best ever? What do I think of Duran still fighting now? All that stuff. The fans were just there to enjoy the event.

There was one guy who came 5,000 miles to get me to sign a programme from Madison Square Garden. He'd been to the Laguna fight in 1971.

One of the things they do when you're inducted into the International Boxing Hall of Fame is make a plaster cast of your fist. Much like what they do with the footprints of the Hollywood legends. The day before my official induction I had my fist cast in plaster. As the plaster was setting I mentioned to the official it was getting hard. He said, 'Just a couple of minutes and it will be ready.'

But behind him were some Scots lads in their kilts waving the Scottish flag and singing. They weren't drunk – just happy to see someone from their own country up on stage being welcomed by the American fans. The official was mesmerised by the tartan and the singing. He started talking to them. I was beginning to think the whole thing was taking too long.

I started to feel that my hand had been in the plaster longer than a couple of minutes. I turned to the official and said the top of the plaster had gone brick hard. 'Shit, man!' he says. 'We'd better get you out now.'

I can see the panic in his eyes. I soon find out why. I try to move and I can't. Fuckin' brilliant! It's the first time I've ever done this, but something tells me it's not going right. I try to free my fingers. Nothing; they're stuck. I try again. It's impossible. I look at the official. 'Move your fingers,' he says. Move them? I could hardly feel them!

'Try to pull your hand out,' he says.

And try as I could, I found it impossible. He tries to pull my arm and hold the bucket with my fist and the plaster in it at the same time. But to no avail. The crowd are starting to get a bit of a laugh out of this. It was like Laurel and Hardy. Another fine mess you've got me into. I asked him if he had a hammer. He didn't. I could see me walking through the customs on my way home.

Anything to declare, sir?

Only this big fuckin' lump of plaster stuck to my fist!

It's getting to the stage where a few of the officials start gathering round me telling me what to do. Pull – push – twist – all the advice you'd expect. One of them even wanted to put his feet on it and get the rest to pull. I had visions of my arm coming right out at the socket. I'm pulling like hell but it won't budge.

I said I would have to put the bucket on the floor where I can get better leverage. 'You can't take it off the table – nobody will see you take your fist out of the plaster,' he says.

I jumped on to the table and started to pull my fist out. It sort of reminded me of all those years ago – 1973 in Copenhagen when I had jumped on to the corner pole during the bout with Miguel Araujo.

I'm pulling and tugging but nothing's happening. The crowd are wondering what I'm doing on the table. Believe you me I never for one minute thought I was going to do it. The official was holding the bucket and pulling at my arm. I had my feet round the bucket tugging like hell. Then finally I felt a bit of movement. 'I can just slightly move my fingers but they feel closed in.'

I pulled and pulled and then I felt it was coming. I was holding my breath as you do when straining. It began to move, slowly. I felt it was on its way, but as I relaxed I felt my fist slide back into the cast. I tried to hold the bucket and pull at the same time, which at last began to help. But as my fist was coming up the gap it came to a halt, as it was bigger than my arm. So I now had to tug like hell to get my fist up through the narrow gap my arm had left. At the same time I had to avoid interfering with the cast of my fist. After a few mighty pulls my whole arm and fist came out. There was a cheer and then an almighty clap from the spectators present, who realised what the problem was. But all I felt was enormous relief. The official, Bob, apologised and blamed it on the Scottish supporters, who had started talking to him when he was staring at their tartan. Thank God the cast was a good one as I didn't want to go through that again.

The final day. I was going through my speech word by word. I was more nervous than going into a world title fight in Madison

Square Garden. Going into a fight I was always confident, but to stand up in front of the world and punch out words was not really my forte. I was very nervous – I felt like I was fighting way out of my class.

Mark and my dad were in the car with me – I had my dad on one side and my son on the other, three generations of Buchanans. We're driving through the cheering crowds. It was amazing. I didn't think for one minute that Mark would be up there with me, but the organisers were great. They knew how to treat a man and how much it would mean to me to have my son and my dad there with me.

This woman came up and she had this wee bairn of about one with her. She asks, 'Ken can I get a photograph taken?'

'Aye, sure, hen. No problem. Geez the bairn.'

I picked up the bairn and she took a photo of me kissing the bairn. That photo ended up all over the papers in America. I felt like a politician; the only difference being that I wasn't trying to score points.

My dad met Gil Clancy and a load of the guys who had been there on our rise to fame. It's all such a blur now – a blur of smiles and crowds and pats on the back. I took my golden Hall of Fame ring and put it on my finger. It weighed much more than I had imagined. It was hard to take in that I was the only living British boxer with one of these things. Then I received my certificate welcoming me into the Hall of Fame. I can't even remember what they said to me. I was shaking when I slipped my speech out of my sporran. I remember the paper shaking as I read it out:

> It is with a sense of immense pride that I stand before you in the presence of such illustrious company both past and present. Most of the high points in my life came during my career as a boxer and it is with this in mind that I would like to take the opportunity to thank everybody who thought me worthy of inclusion in this ceremony today.

Acknowledgement of achievement should always be welcome. I (as I am sure we all are) am deeply honoured by this accolade. I would also like to thank the members of the International Boxing Hall of Fame without whom none of this would be possible. It is through the work of such organisations that the spirit of sport survives and flourishes. Ed Brophy and his corner do an excellent job and I applaud their efforts.

I have travelled a good few miles to get here. And now as I stand before you my thoughts drift back across the sea to all my family and friends back home. Scotland is a small nation and it is my hope that this award will add something to its already growing reputation both in Great Britain and abroad.

All that is left for me to say is a special heartfelt thank you to the man who, above all else, helped mould me into the champion I was to become. That man is of course my dad, Tommy.

I could never express fully in words my debt of gratitude to him. Suffice to say, my mother and himself gave me life. Throughout that life he has always been there. Sometimes as a dad – sometimes as a trainer – but always as a friend. Thanks, Dad.

Once again thank you all. And God bless America.

I can assure you there did not seem to be a dry eye in the hall. I didn't realise how much the words I said would affect people, but they came from the heart. I was glad it went down so well. The whole day was filled with nostalgia in more ways than one. Seeing all these former and present world champions gathered together having a laugh and telling stories took me back.

Carlos Ortiz told me how in 1972 he was matched with Roberto Duran at Madison Square Garden. Duran pulled out five days before the fight, having hurt his hand. The promoters got in touch with me. I was on holiday in the Channel Islands with my wife and son Mark who was coming up for two. Promoter Teddy Brenner pleaded with me on the phone on three occasions to step in. In the first two conversations I told him no way was I going to face Ortiz. Ortiz was no mug – he had made a comeback at welterweight and had won ten out of ten fights since. Not only that – nine of them were by knockout.

Then by the third time Teddy Brenner rang I gave in. The funny side of Carlos's story is that when he was told he was boxing me instead of Duran he insisted on being paid $10,000 more. He said I was a harder opponent than Duran. This was after I had lost my title to Duran. Aye! There's more to boxing than throwing punches. But thanks Carlos – it was nice of you to mention that. Now that I think about it, I wish I had held out for more money myself!

I also met Ruben Olivares. I was talking away to him for about ten minutes and all he did was nod his head or occasionally say *si*, but I was getting into the swing of it. Eventually, this guy comes up and says to me, 'I'm Ruben's interpreter. He does not speak any English.'

You can imagine the idiot I felt, as Ruben was laughing away. I had to laugh. What else can you do?

afterword

I suppose I do have some real regrets about my life. My regrets, I suppose, are ordinary ones. Regrets we'll all have whether we were champion of the world or not. My biggest one is losing my mum, Cathy, so young. She was only fifty-one and never got to see me winning a world title. Because my dad was older than your usual dad he had wisdom. He used that to bring us up as pals rather than being a strict father. He was – and still is – more like a brother to me than a father. I suppose that is the aim of all fathers. My dad never lifted his hands to me or my brother. That in itself was unusual in the times I grew up, when it was acceptable for parents to hit their kids. His life was his two sons. I've always been a bit explosive. My dad tried to help me to keep the lid on that. He was a calming influence on my life. He was at my training sessions every day – he *was* my trainer, basically. Trainer – mentor – advisor – father – friend.

Looking back, I truly realise how helpful my dad has been to me. Not just as a dad, or trainer, or companion, but as my best friend. Both of us were thrown in at the deep end. When I turned professional in 1965 my dad had to sign my contract because I was underage. There were times when things went wrong, I would blame my dad. In actual fact, I was usually the one who made the mistake.

My dad would ask me to find out from Eddie Thomas how much money I'd be getting for the next fight. I would fob him off saying I didn't want to pester Eddie about financial matters. My dad would never push the question further. In all honesty, I never knew how much I was getting for my upcoming fight. The first time I knew how much my purse would be was when I challenged Maurice Cullen for his British lightweight title in 1968.

I was trying to keep both Eddie and my dad happy, and what with all the training, fight and press conferences I felt I had enough on my plate already.

I have never asked any other boxer if they were in the same position as myself. I would advise any young lad who was just about to turn professional to make sure they know how much they are earning and where every penny has gone.

Now I am fifty-five and I look back on my career with pride. I have truly fulfilled my ambition, an ambition born when I was an eight-year-old boy way back in 1953. There is no taking the fact away that I was champion of the world. The whole bloody world! I've been recognised by the boxing fraternity all over the world when I was inducted into the International Boxing Hall of Fame, and in October 2000 I will be inducted into the Los Angeles Boxing Hall of Fame along with my old pal Barry McGuigan.

We're all fighters, every single one of us. Fighting is the first sport of every man and woman. From the minute we're born, we're fighting to breathe. Then we're fighting to open our eyes. We're fighting to walk and we're fighting to talk. You can't get rid of your desire to fight when that is the very first lesson in life.

professional career record

Born Edinburgh, 28 June 1945
Record: 69 bouts, 61 won (inc. 27 KOs), 8 lost

Date	Opponent	Location	Result	Round	Stoppage
20/9/65	Brian Tonks	London	Won	2	KO
18/10/65	Vic Woodhall	Manchester	Won	2	KO
1/11/65	Billy Williams	London	Won	3	KO
22/11/65	Joe Okezie	London	Won	3	KO
13/12/65	Junior Cassidy	London	Won	8	PTS
24/1/66	Tommy Tiger	London	Won	8	PTS
7/3/66	Manley Brown	London	Won	4	KO
4/4/66	Tommy Tiger	London	Won	8	PTS
19/4/66	Chris Elliot	Manchester	Won	8	PTS
11/5/66	Junior Cassidy	Manchester	Won	8	PTS
12/7/66	Brian Smith	Aberdeen	Won	1	KO
6/8/66	Ivan Whitter	London	Won	8	PTS
6/9/66	Mick Laud	London	Won	8	PTS
17/10/66	Antonio Paiva	London	Won	10	PTS
29/11/66	Al Keen	Leeds	Won	8	PTS
19/12/66	Phil Lundgren	London	Won	10	PTS
23/1/67	John McMillan	Glasgow	Won	10	PTS
14/2/67	Tommy Garrison	London	Won	10	PTS
11/5/67	Franco Brondi	Paisley	Won	3	KO
28/6/67	Winston Laud	London	Won	8	PTS
26/7/67	Rene Roque	Aberdeen	Won	10	PTS
14/9/67	Al Rocca	London	Won	7	KO
30/10/67	Jim McCormack	London	Won	12	PTS

Date	Opponent	Location	Result	Round	Stoppage
19/2/68	Maurice Cullen (for British lightweight title)	London	Won	11	KO
22/4/68	Leonard Tavarez	London	Won	8	PTS
10/6/68	Ivan Whitter	London	Won	8	PTS
23/10/68	Angel Robinson Garcia	Mayfair	Won	10	PTS
11/12/68	Ameur Lamine	Hamilton	Won	3	KO
2/1/69	Frankie Narvaez	Piccadilly	Won	10	PTS
17/2/69	Mike Cruz	Mayfair	Won	5	KO
5/3/69	Jose Luis Torcida	Solihull	Won	10	PTS
14/7/69	Jerry Gracy	Nottingham	Won	1	KO
11/11/69	Vincenzo Pitardi	Mayfair	Won	2	KO
29/1/70	Miguel Velazquez (for European lightweight title)	Madrid	Lost	15	PTS
23/2/70	Leonard Tavarez	Piccadilly	Won	10	PTS
6/4/70	Chris Fernandez	Nottingham	Won	10	PTS
12/5/70	Brian Hudson (for British lightweight title)	London	Won	5	KO
26/9/70	Ismael Laguna (for World lightweight title)	San Juan, Puerto Rico	Won	15	PTS
7/12/70	Donato Paduano	New York	Won	10	PTS
12/2/71	Ruben Navarro (for World lightweight title)	Los Angeles	Won	15	PTS
10/5/71	Carlos Hernandez	London	Won	8	KO
13/9/71	Ismael Laguna (for World lightweight title)	Madison Square Garden	Won	15	PTS
28/3/72	Al Ford	London	Won	10	PTS
29/4/72	Andries Steyn	Johannesburg	Won	3	KO
26/6/72	Roberto Duran (for World lightweight title)	New York	Lost	14	KO
20/9/72	Carlos Ortiz	New York	Won	7	KO
4/12/72	Chang Kil Lee	New York	Won	2	KO
29/1/73	Jim Watt (for British lightweight title)	Glasgow	Won	15	PTS
27/3/73	Hector Matta	London	Won	10	PTS
29/5/73	Frankie Otero	Miami Beach	Won	10	PTS
1/9/73	Edwin Malave	New York	Won	7	KO
11/10/73	Frankie Otero	Toronto	Won	6	KO
6/12/73	Miguel Araujo	Copenhagen	Won	1	KO
7/2/74	José Peterson	Copenhagen	Won	10	PTS

Date	Opponent	Location	Result	Round	Stoppage
4/4/74	Joe Tetteh	Copenhagen	Won	3	KO
1/5/74	Antonio Puddu (for European lightweight title)	Cagliari, Italy	Won	6	KO
21/11/74	Winston Noel	Copenhagen	Won	2	KO
16/12/74	Leonard Tavarez (for European lightweight title)	Paris	Won	14	KO
27/2/75	Ishimatsu Suzuki (for WBC lightweight title)	Tokyo	Lost	15	PTS
25/7/75	Giancarlo Usai (for European lightweight title)	Cagliari, Italy	Won	12	KO
28/6/79	Benny Benitez	Randers, Denmark	Won	8	PTS
6/9/79	Eloi de Souza	Randers, Denmark	Won	8	PTS
6/12/79	Charlie Nash (for European lightweight title)	Copenhagen	Lost	12	PTS
15/5/80	Najib Daho	London	Won	7	KO
20/10/80	Des Gwilliam	Birmingham	Won	8	PTS
26/1/81	Steve Early	Edgbaston	Lost	12	PTS
4/4/81	Langton Tinago	Salisbury	Lost	10	PTS
24/11/81	Lance Williams	London	Lost	8	PTS
25/1/82	George Feeney	Piccadilly	Lost	8	PTS

index